WRITE A
SUCCESSFUL
NOVEL

WRITE A
SUCCESSFUL
NOVEL

Frederick E Smith
Best selling author of 633 SQUADRON, etc
and
Moe Sherrard-Smith
Adjudicator, editor, literary agent

 Escreet Publications

To the many readers, students, would-be novelists, and fellow authors from whose interest this book was born

First published 1991

Published by
Escreet Publications
Garthend House,
Millington,
York YO4 2TX

© 1991 Frederick E Smith
© 1991 Moe Sherrard-Smith

British Library Cataloguing in Publication Data
  Smith, Frederick E
    Write a successful novel
    I. Title II. Sherrard-Smith, Moe
    808.042

    ISBN 0 9517623 0 3

Text set in English Times
from Amstrad PCW 9512 disc

Printed in England by
Roman Press Limited, Bournemouth

Contents

PART TWO

PART THREE

Introduction

Would-be novelists are full of questions: from the nuts and bolts of the craft's technique to the problems of submission to agents or publishers.

We who are authors, assessors and lecturers are constantly asked for advice and opinions on that all important question: "How do I write a novel?" This question comes even more repeatedly from the students of my WRITING TUTORIAL.

As the award-winning author of thirty-five novels, many of which have been sold to film companies, Frederick E Smith is likewise besieged by writers seeking advice and help. When wearing my journalist's hat, I have the task of asking questions and eliciting information, and it was in this role that I interviewed Frederick E Smith about his life and times as a novelist, putting to him many of the questions my students ask me.

His answers, his comments on the mechanics of the craft, and the chronicles of his struggles against the variety of obstacles surrounding both would-be and established authors, proved to be a fascinating and informative revelation. Because he is a writer whose knowledge has been gained entirely from hard experience, and because his novels range from thrillers to subjects as consequential as apartheid, modern revolution, and the conflict between sex and love, his comments had a sharpness and realism very different from those of people who attempt to teach creative writing without such a rich background.

Some of his remarks were undoubtedly controversial but all of them immensely informative and it occurred to me what a great source of help they would be to a novice in guiding him through the jungle of writing and publishing.

Because of this I asked him if he would agree to the publication of these questions and answers in a book on the art of writing the novel. At first he refused, feeling that if he were asked to comment on other authors' work, it would be presumptuous for a third party to insist he knew other men's motivations better than those authors themselves.

Holding the same views, I insisted that he used only his own novels to illustrate his answers, works that he feels totally qualified to dissect and criticise. At the same time I insisted that he did not let false modesty dilute their value. This is the reason that throughout this book I have asked him direct questions about his own novels.

This book is the result. In it you will embark on a journey that covers every aspect of novel writing. You will learn how ideas are obtained; the difference between theme and plot; how plots are developed and turned into full length novels. You will learn how to present those novels to their best advantage and the ways a new novelist should go about marketing his work.

Equally importantly, you will learn Frederick E Smith's best selling secrets; how he has trained his mind to cope with the problems and the strain of novel writing; how he handles research; how personal experience has taught him to handle agents and publishers. You will also learn, from his own honestly expressed personal comments, how to distinguish between good agents and publishers and bad ones. And you will learn about the inevitable conflicts that occur when the worlds of art and business come into contact.

An additional fascination are the anecdotes from his adventures when researching his novels. Some are very exciting, for he is an author who has never spared himself in his search for the truth.

You will, therefore, learn in the author's own words, and by examples from his books, the way he approaches his craft. From the chapter-end illustrations, you will be offered a unique opportunity to share in an author's creative process. By studying the progress from plot idea, through structure and groundwork, to the finished product, you will understand the craftsmanship behind the creation of Frederick E Smith's powerful novel about love and guilt, OF MASKS AND MINDS.

His life as a novelist has been a highly successful adventure and by turning these pages you can share in that adventure while you also learn its secrets. This is a book that will fascinate anyone interested in the way a writer's mind works, and a must for anyone who aspires to be a novelist.

Moe Sherrard-Smith

I saw Moe Sherrard-Smith's point that, having lectured over the years on the art of creating a novel, putting my experience into writing was the next logical step, given the growing numbers of requests from students for a book to reinforce my lectures.

From that step, therefore, grew this book, and its distinct format evolved from Moe Sherrard-Smith's recognition of its value as a working aid for would-be writers.

By drawing on her considerable experience in assessing manuscripts and teaching creative writing, she has been able to highlight the problematic areas for students, and ask the probing questions that have, at times, caused me to consider more deeply certain aspects of novel writing. That inner questioning has, in turn, enabled me to present a fuller reflection on the process than proves possible during lectures.

I am indebted to her for organising the subject matter and my (quite often chaotic) notes into their appropriate order, and prompting me to look back over the process of creating my novel OF MASKS AND MINDS for the Illustrations. That has been a kind of adventure for me, and one in which I hope you will gladly share.

Frederick E Smith

As this book is written to help novelists, it is unashamedly written from their point of view and not from the viewpoint of their agents and publishers who are, it is felt, more able to take care of themselves.

Throughout the book, the pronoun 'he' has been employed to encompass both male and female would-be novelists, rather than constant reference to the cumbersome 'he or she' substitute which would make for tedious reading.

Part One

1 *The Novel and The Novelist*

Novel writing is your main vocation. The dictionary would define the novel as 'an extended work in prose' but there is obviously more to it than that. With your wide experience in the field, how would you define a novel?

No literary work is more flexible - perhaps that is why, in spite of the cynics who keep writing it off as dead, the novel remains with us as vigorous as ever. It cannot be said to be entirely about people - novels have had horses, dogs, cats, rabbits and even cars and aircraft as their heroes. But although such stories are labelled as novels and sold as such, I would prefer to talk about novels as dealing with people: about their hopes and fears, their loves and hates, their good deeds and the evil deeds they commit on one another and on the world.

The tendency nowadays seems to be towards specialisation, the so-called 'market slot' labelling. As it would be an impossible task to try to categorise your versatile range into any one market slot, you presumably don't subscribe to that kind of policy. Do you have strong feelings about the kind of novel a writer should attempt?

For me a novel should be the kind of book I *want* to write. Not what others say I should write and eventually specialise in. I dislike intensely the way salesmen and accountants have persuaded publishers, bookshops, the public and, even worse, writers themselves, to believe that a novelist is only at his best when he writes one kind of novel. I believe a good creative writer can weave a novel around almost any subject, as the 19th and early 20th century novelists often did, provided he is prepared to go to the trouble of doing the research.

The catch here, of course, is why should novelists go to this trouble when their publishers practically insist on them writing the same kind of book over and over again? So many take the easy route and never find out if they would have been better novelists writing in other fields.

You are saying, then, that your kind of versatility can be detrimental, given the current climate in publishing. With your own books, for instance, there would be a FREDERICK E SMITH on virtually every genre shelf and not all cosily clustered for display convenience. Isn't it true to say that versatility has almost become a dirty word?

I have to agree. An author today who tries to extend his frontiers is very likely to pay a heavy price for it. Publishers, who like a writer to seize one small corner of the market with his particular type of novel and hold it for the rest of his writing life, will grumble and quite often terminate an association with a novelist if he insists on trying something else. It has happened to me half a dozen times, so I'm well qualified to talk about it.

So it isn't a practice you would recommend to a beginner?

I can't go that far, seeing I did it when I was a beginner and have continued to do so all my writing life. So much depends on the writer, whether or not he is ambitious enough to take the risks. Eventually I've always sold my rejected books somewhere (even though in each case I had to begin again at the bottom of the advance royalty ladder) so I must stick to my belief that every writer should write about the things he feels deeply about, because then he will produce his best work.

If a writer does this, then his novels are bound to vary greatly in theme and content because I've always found that born writers have many interests. In a way I think of them as expensive radio sets with many frequencies on their wave bands. When they first take up writing they often have one paramount subject they want to dramatise. But once this compulsive book has been written, other themes take its place as the writer, always a seeker of knowledge, widens and develops his interests. It is these themes that keep his work fresh and enthusiastic.

But not as profitable in terms of royalties as keeping to the same successful formula?

I suppose we are really talking here about what a novelist wants out of his writing. If he wants simply to make money, then there is no question it is more lucrative to keep writing the same kind of book once the first one has been successful. Not only will this please his publisher, it will be easier and quicker to write than his having to research an entirely different subject.

This isn't to suggest for one moment that I look down on writers who work for money alone. Just about everyone else works for money, so why shouldn't a writer? My point is simply that if he wants to achieve his *best work,* I believe he achieves it by writing about things that inspire or inflame him, always provided he doesn't let his enthusiasm unbalance his novel. Fiction, remember, is about emotion and the more deeply one feels about something, the greater will be the vitality in the finished work. And vitality is so important in writing.

A writer might not, I repeat, make as much money out of his work if he keeps on changing his themes, but the compensation will be that he has continued saying the things that he wants to say and done his artistic best in saying them, and to some writers that is the greatest satisfaction of all.

Assuming, then, that a novelist has decided not to restrict himself to a particular type of book, how would you equate this with advice often given to writers that they should 'study the market'? For someone facing the daunting task of putting pen to paper on a work that may be years in the creation, forecasting which publisher wants what, and in which style, must surely be akin to looking into a crystal ball?

Market study is good advice if he is writing articles or short stories for magazines because these are short term projects that do not call for huge investments in time and energy. They are also published relatively quickly after they are written, and before a publisher's tastes and requirements have had time to change.

A novel is a different kind of race altogether. It is not a sprint, it is a marathon. One has to write on, day after day, week after week, month after month, in health, in sickness, and sometimes in downright misery. To keep going a writer needs motivation and what better motivation is there than writing about something that interests or excites him?

Of course I'm fully aware that in his early days, a writer's desire to be published can be enough of a motivation in itself. But even then he should ignore the trendy themes that appear to be making authors plenty of money (but often aren't). For one thing these themes are likely to be quite wrong for him. For another, it takes two, three, or even more years for a novel to be written, printed, and to appear in the bookshops, and by then public taste will almost certainly have changed and the demand for that theme might have disappeared.

On the other hand, a theme that excites a beginner will do two things if kept under control. It will produce a higher class of work because the emotion he feels will produce vitality, and it will also provide the motivation that will keep him going and help him to surmount the daily drudgery of life. The novel might lack skilful construction and characterisation at that early point in his career but then so would any other kind of book he might have written. All things being equal it will have a better chance of acceptance because it will have that critical ingredient, vitality. Remember that word. It can transform a poor novel into a great one.

You are saying that if a writer can transmit his vitality into the writing it can transform even a mediocre work into a powerful book that people will be eager to read?

Most certainly. I have often cited Wuthering Heights as an example. The plot is amateurish and clumsy, the characters melodramatic, but the novel is still a great one because of the enormous frustrated vitality contained in almost every word. Write a novel with that kind of power and any publisher worth his salt will fall over backwards to take it.

Of course there can be other motivations. A powerful one is need. The rent and gas bill to pay, hungry mouths to feed, things like this seldom fail to keep one's typewriter clicking. With motivation of this kind a man can turn his hand to almost any kind of novel and find the incentive to work hard.

Isn't that at conflict with your earlier statement that an author produces a better book under the influence of his own burning ambition to write about a subject? Will 'need' provide sufficient energy if one isn't particularly interested in a subject?

Ironically it is usually the very time that one picks on a powerful theme because nothing else can match one's emotions.

But it's not a way of kindling energy that you would recommend?

No. One has to be masochistic enough to burn one's bridges and leave oneself with no other income. Having been through that fire, I would not recommend it to my worst enemy.

I presume you're referring to your early days when, fired with the ambition to become a professional writer, you left a good post overseas and returned to Britain almost penniless. That must have been challenging but very stressful?

It was stressful, and because of that I can't recommend that a beginner gives up his job until his foothold as a writer is secure. (If writers are ever secure!) Also, not everyone can work under that kind of stress. Some panic and their work suffers accordingly. Far better motivation comes from subjects that interest, anger, or stimulate one. On the positive side, that stimulation might be love of children, religion, a passion for flying, a belief in the supernatural, or even nostalgia for one's golden years. On the negative side, it might be a hatred of atomic weapons, of apartheid, of war or class consciousness.

Everything I have just said applies equally to genre novels. If a novelist's greater interest is in detective, mystery, war, or romantic novels, then these are the stories he should write first. In some writers this interest might occupy his entire writing life. If it does, who am I to say the writer is wrong if he fulfils himself and pleases both his publisher and his readers?

But I stick to my guns that if a writer has a number of interests he ought to write about them. Another reason is the challenge they offer, and that can be a motivation too. After my first three novels, which I wrote in the 3rd person, I decided I would like to write one in the 1st person, and through the eyes of a woman.

That novel would be your highly successful LYDIA TRENDEN-NIS, so skilfully done that many readers find it difficult to accept it was written by a man?

I can't claim that but it certainly proved to be the best gamble I ever made. WOMAN bought the serial rights, RANK bought the film rights, and to date the book has sold in over thirty countries. In fact, after thirty years, it is still selling somewhere in the world. If I had taken the advice of my publisher and stuck with the 3rd person and male viewpoint, none of that would have happened.

As I said earlier, this is the point where a writer and his publisher might clash. If the writer finds the present formula is beginning to bore him and he refuses to continue with it, the publisher might well decide to strike him off his list. It is a difficult choice for an author to face and no one can blame him if he tries to continue with a genre in which he is accepted and successful. My advice, however, would always be to keep with subjects that excite him because in that way his work will remain fresh and vigorous.

I've gone on at some length about the need of a writer to be his own master in his choice of subject because today more than ever authors, promising ones and established ones alike, are being bullied by their publishers or their agents to write about this and that subject, and to put this and that into their work. I'm not suggesting one shouldn't listen to a good editor when he suggests a better turn of phrase, a better incident, or, in extreme cases, even the need of another character. But for all the reasons I've just mentioned, I do suggest an author should think twice when an editor suggests a theme and how to handle it. The author is the artist: the publisher or agent is not, and an artist should always be true to himself.

There seems to be no shortage of people anxious to take up novel writing, but even among those with talent there are many who either don't finish a book or don't make the grade even if they do. What is it they lack?

They lack determination: the ability to stick at the work day in and day out and to sacrifice social and/or family life on the altar of self-discipline. If a person hasn't this quality, the desire to write a novel, either because he feels he 'has a book in him', or because it's the 'in thing to do', won't be enough to ensure success even if he has talent. There is no escaping the unglamorous daily (and often nightly) slog at pen or typewriter.

Self-discipline and determination will keep the pen to the paper, but won't the novice fail at the final hurdle if he doesn't have, or doesn't cultivate, the severest form of self-criticism?

Most certainly he will. And it is one of the hardest things to cultivate because it involves objectivity. Every writer has moments when words flow from his pen almost as if they were coming from a spiritual scribe. While they come, it seems not to matter that they are almost irrelevant to the story-line: they seem works of art in themselves. For a writer to recognise their superfluity takes both discernment and strength of character.

This power of self-criticism applies to almost every element in a novel. A writer has to put himself into the skin of someone who in the beginning knows little or nothing about the plot and even less about the characters. But who is this someone to be? A discerning reader or an unimaginative one? If he chooses the first, a writer might leave out too much detail; if he chooses the latter he might put too much in.

He will try, of course, to settle on an average reader but who will that be? A man, a woman, a happy soul, a melancholy soul, a rich man, a poor man, an Englishman, an American? There is no way one can identify an average reader and so the writer is finally compelled to use himself as the guinea pig.

So he has to be schizophrenic, with one part of him viewing the book he knows so intimately as if he had never seen it before. This isn't easy, and even if it is achieved, the writer can never be sure that his judgement is valid.

But there is no other course open to him. To ask friends to read the final work can be fatal because, unless they are experts at novel assessments, the closeness of the relationship almost always lends itself to a bias one way or the other.

This need to be acutely self-critical is often the reason why otherwise talented writers fail in their ambition. If a novice writer knows he has this weakness, he would be well advised to look for a different career.

It's hard work, stressful, a lonely occupation. Why do you choose to write novels?

I don't think I can give a clear-cut answer to that. There might be half a dozen reasons. Certainly I've always enjoyed reading novels for their entertainment value alone. But I've also been impressed by the novel's power to influence public opinion and overcome prejudice. I'm thinking of the social effects of books like Uncle Tom's Cabin, and the novels of Dickens, Faulkner and Steinbeck.

Fiction has other assets too. Many people live such humdrum lives that they have little chance to learn about the complexity of human nature. Good fiction gives them the opportunity to view its many moods and guises, and as most writers use some personal experience in their work, books offer a richer and cheaper lesson on human nature than any psychologist can provide. That is why in many countries, with the possible exception of England and the United States, fiction is regarded as the most difficult and most important branch of literature. I draw comfort from that whenever people ask me what I write and they give that familiar but disparaging grunt - Fiction? Oh!

Nevertheless I'm sure you'll concede that there are many beginners who haven't any windmills they want to tilt at but just simply want to write a novel. What do they do?

I'll go further and say that there are many who haven't even got an idea for one. Let me say at once that they are not alone. Most of us have been in the same situation and most of us will get into that situation again. This is the time when it's important to know the difference between theme and plot and to know where to seek ideas.

ILLUSTRATION 1: Do I really want to write?

There are many reasons for choosing to write, and many areas available.

Knowing that you *want* to write is of first importance, knowing *what* comes second.

To know you *want* to write, ask yourself:

Do I have determination and staying power?
Can I finish a hard task, or do I give up?
Can I work long hours, often (or preferably) alone?
Have I a burning compulsion to communicate my ideas?

Knowing *what* to write often comes from personal choice.

Do I want to write novels or short stories?
Do I want to write general novels or a specialised genre.

In the chapters and illustrations that follow, you can explore the creation and the publication of a novel. It is not always possible to describe in text the creative thought processes that underpin any form of fiction writing and the end of chapter illustrations are provided to give insight into the development and expansion of a basic idea.

In glimpses from the notebook jottings, you can watch the novel begin to grow - like a time-lapsed scan of foetal development. Just as a child is conceived, grows in the womb, and inevitably makes its debut in the wider arena of life, so a novel is created and published.

2 *Theme and Plot*

Many students, asked for the 'theme' (or subject) of their novel give a lengthy run down of the plot. Others, asked for the 'plot' (or story-line) provide little more than two sentences of theme. We are speaking here of two different things and how they inter-relate. How would you define this difference between theme and plot?

They are often confused but are quite different things. The theme is the influence, concept, subject, or emotion that motivates one to write a novel. Every novel has a theme, though in the lighter books it is often little more than a definition of its genre: western, romance, war, etc. As novels grow in stature, the themes become more defined and important. It might be sexual jealousy, dislike of nuclear weapons, snobbery, or racism. The writer has decided to make a case for or against whichever theme he has chosen and to make this case he is not going in the pulpit, not writing to The Times, but instead he is using the medium of drama, in this case the novel.

There is an essential value in knowing the theme when writing a novel. It acts as a kind of railway line or track that keeps the novelist from losing his way. In my early days I sometimes wrote novels without giving thought to their theme and, despite having worked out a plot, found myself struggling with the problems of how to continue and develop the characters. It was only when I paused and made myself define the novel's theme that I was able to see the purpose of my characters more clearly and allow them to play their full part in the story.

We've already established that you like a powerful theme for your novels. But you also admitted that sometimes you thought of a plot first and then recognised the theme later. In a book like THE TORMENTED, which came first, the chicken or the egg?

I thought of the basic idea or plot first. That was in 1959 and it excited me tremendously. In fact I doubted if I would ever think of a better one. (One can boast about ideas because they seem to come from outside one's mind. What one can't boast about is how they are handled: that is a matter of one's skill or lack of it.) Because I thought so highly of the idea, I decided I wasn't fully equipped to handle it, because at that time I had only published five novels.

So I let the idea simmer in my mind for ten years while I wrote other books, always afraid someone else might use the idea before me. In 1969, although I still doubted my qualifications, I decided it was too risky to wait any longer and I commenced the writing.

By that time, however, I had long discovered its main theme and that excited me as much as the idea itself. It was the problem I felt all pacifists must face. Although they might have the courage and will-power to turn the other cheek when attacked, what are their obligations when they encounter some innocent person being violated? If they are physically capable of intervention, should they remain true to their pacifist belief or should they give help? This theme excited me enough to keep me working for three years on the novel.

Were you satisfied with it after all that preliminary work?

More than I usually am. No novel, no creative work of any kind can equal the original golden image in the writer's mind. Too much is lost because of the inadequacies of one's language, and because of the image's transmission through muscle, bone, sinew, and typewriter to the page. This loss happens to all forms of art and is the reason no true artist is ever satisfied with his work. I usually estimate 50 per cent of the original image is lost. In this book I believe I had lost only 30 per cent.

Which came first in THE SIN AND THE SINNERS?

The theme. I once knew a family who adopted a child as simply a plaything for their natural offspring, and having seen the consequences on the adopted child, I had to make it the theme of a novel.

At this point I must say that not every novelist will agree that a strong theme is necessary in a novel and it is quite true that some excellent novels have been written without one. The same novelists will argue that a novel's main function is to entertain and I'll agree with that also. Nevertheless, I still argue there is no better way of introducing vitality into one's work than by writing of something one feels strongly about. I also believe it helps any writer to know what the theme of his novel is (because every novel does have one), even if its influence on his plot is minimal.

Of course a writer does not let theme intrude as crudely as it sounds here. On the contrary, it has to be handled extremely subtly or the reader will resent being preached at and will throw the book down.

Surely, though, if a writer uses a theme he is anxious to convey, there is a great risk that he will thrust it down a reader's throat. How does he temper his crusade in his novel?

By skilful plotting. Plot is a dramatisation of the theme. For this dramatisation a writer needs good characters; good dialogue; situations that bring out the best or the worse aspects of his theme; and a story-line that has enough entertainment to keep a reader glued to the book and unaware an influence is being exerted on him.

To construct such a plot, conflict, suspense, and sometimes mystery are essential. Conflict provides the stress on the water that makes eddies, whirlpools, currents, and waterfalls. A story about totally contented people would not be a story at all. Nor would it be true to life. If people do not have outer conflicts, they have inner ones. It is the use of one or the other (or both) that provide the situations from which the plot is built.

If recognition of a theme should come after a book is started, mightn't this sometimes change the entire story-line or dimension of a novel? Has this ever been your experience?

Yes, it has. In my novel THE WAR GOD, my original idea was to write a novel about the deserters in Italy during World War Two. These men, a mixture of all the races who fought in that country, banded together in the mountains and used to raid the supply columns of both Allies and Germans alike. Indeed, they were such a nuisance that when Allied and German patrols went out searching for the deserters, the patrols were ordered not to fire on one another.

This true life situation seemed to me to have the makings of a good adventure story and after working out a plot involving a band of such men, with a charismatic German leader, I took it to my publishers and obtained a commission to write the book. It was only when I began the actual writing and started asking myself what the theme was, that new ideas came to me.

As things stood at first, the theme was merely greed and self-interest. But what if it were changed into something less simplistic, such as altruism and a hatred of war? Supposing I made my German leader into a man who hated the destruction that the Allied and German armies were inflicting on innocent Italian communities? With men from all nationalities in his band, he would be in an ideal position to infiltrate either army and learn its plans. With this knowledge he might be able to save villages from destruction.

Of course I could not invest his men with these high ideals. He had to shape their activities so that they still received their plunder, while at the same time those activities stymied first one army and then the other from inflicting serious damage on the countryside. If, for example, the Germans were planning to blow up a dam to hold up the advance of the Allies, he could tip off the Allies so that they could take counter measures. And vice versa. In other words the German, ahead of his time in believing war could only be prevented by international police action, would be using his little army as an advance United Nations unit. And if at the end of the story I could somehow contrive an ironical situation in which he and his band of criminals defend and save an Italian village from destruction by holding off a collision of the two armies, what an anti-war novel it could become!

It meant that the plot-line had to be changed quite considerably to add ambiguity to some of the German leader's actions, but it all became worthwhile when it lifted what had previously been a mere adventure story into one with a strong anti-war message. The new plot also allowed a much deeper character study of the leader himself, adding a mystery element to some of his operations, which would have been totally lacking in the first version.

At the same time, none of the excitement of the first version was lost. The raids on convoys still continued: the only difference being the reason for them, and even that became known only deep into the story. In fact, with this new theme in mind, I was able to create more exciting situations than had existed in the earlier plot. It became a very satisfying novel to complete, particularly after a critic called it the only war novel with a moral he had ever read.

SUB PLOTS

So far plot has embraced the overall structure of a novel as a single entity. Are there occasions when it is necessary to construct sub-plots within that framework?

Yes, often. Few stories have a single plot-line. More often than not sub-plots are necessary to establish the relationship between characters or to explain why a certain situation has come about. This applies to most novels although the more complex the story, the more likely they are to occur.

In the past, when there were fewer calls on the leisure time of their readers, writers would throw in sub-plots that had hardly any bearing at all on the main story-line. In other words they were stories within stories, often with the only link being the names of the characters. The purpose was to produce a bigger read for the customer's money. With the exceptions of certain blockbusters, this is seldom done today. The novel is much more streamlined and sure-footed.

Are you saying that in modern literature a sub-plot must have an integral bearing on the major plot?

Not quite. There will always be the exception that proves the rule. But in the vast majority of modern novels sub-plots have a definite purpose. They add weight to characters, explain situations, advance the main story-line, and give the novel balance. If we think of its trunk as the main plot-line, a tree is a useful comparison here. Perhaps it might just survive without branches, but how thin, sterile and uninteresting it would be. Let it grow branches, however, and it can blossom, bear fruit and have symmetry. A novel needs sub-plots for the same reasons.

Can you give an example from your own work?

I used sub-plots a great deal in my 633 SQUADRON series. In OPERATION RHINE MAIDEN I had a young girl who lived in terror every time her husband, a navigator called Marsh, flew out on a mission. In turn her fear affected Marsh to the point he feared death not for himself but because he believed Julie, his wife, would never be able to survive without him.

This story was woven into the mainstream plot and served a number of purposes. It showed the strain air crews lived under; it enabled me to show the perils of the missions my story encompassed; and when I brought the sub-plot to a climax by Marsh's aircraft being crippled over Germany, it not only emphasised the protective nature of one of my main characters, but also provided an intermediate crisis that gave greater power and impetus to the main story-line.

Thus, when carefully chosen, sub-plots can have enormous value to a novel both in providing additional interest to the reader and in advancing the story itself.

You must have experienced at some time plots which appear quite promising initially, but don't or can't work. At what stage should the struggle be abandoned?

Yes, I've been disappointed with ideas that at first seemed promising and I'm sure most writers have. Although one tends to develop an instinct for what is suitable and what isn't, sometimes it isn't possible to be certain until a synopsis has been attempted. Whatever the waste in time and effort, this should always be done because it's far better to find out the unsuitability of an idea at this early stage than when one is halfway through the novel itself.

A word of advice here, however. Never throw away or forget an idea. Sometimes they only need an extra element, perhaps a new character or a new slant, to make them viable. In the strange way the mind works, one might think of these elements months or even years later. That might bring the entire project back to life again.

FINDING IDEAS

What of the person who has a burning desire to write, but lacks a compelling theme and hasn't any plot ideas? Where does he find an idea that excites him?

Firstly he mustn't give up heart, because themes and plot ideas are all around him. But until he has trained his mind, he won't see them. Among the best sources are the tabloid newspapers. They cover the entire seedy spectrum of life with all its traumas and dramas.

Wasn't this how your second novel, OF MASKS AND MINDS, came into being, from news of an experimental operation?

Yes, there was a small article about a famous scientist who needed a particular type of brain operation that could save his sanity but might also destroy his creative faculties.

This idea, being picked up from a newspaper, was not inspired by any burning theme and so would seem to contradict what I said earlier about the usefulness of having one. The truth was I found the idea exciting enough in itself to provide vitality - not to mention my being desperate to earn money at that stage in my career. But, of course, there was a theme and as soon as I recognised it, I was greatly helped in developing my characters more fully and sympathetically. The theme was a love so deep and understanding that a woman was prepared to sacrifice her own happiness for the artistic creativity that was her husband's life.

So although a story-line can apparently be created without a theme to inspire it, a theme will almost always be discovered when either the synopsis is being constructed or the novel itself is being written. Conversely, if a writer begins with a theme and designs a plot from it, the basic rules about plot structure remain exactly the same. He still needs all the construction elements I have just mentioned, no matter what kind of novel he intends to write.

Newspapers, the Agony Aunt letters in women's magazines, even The Bible, are all rich sources to trigger ideas. Any more suggestions?

Yes, there is personal experience, one's own philosophy and obsessions, new inventions, conversations overheard at work, on the bus or in the supermarket queue, social and political upheavals, sporting successes or failures, characters whose adventures you'd like to share (and can share if you write about similar events) - the list is almost endless. A writer should be receptive to all the stimuli around him and store away everything of interest for future use.

I recommend to my students the use of an Ideas Book or file, so that no thought ever escapes. Would you do the same?

Most certainly. As I suggested earlier, one should never throw away ideas, nor for that matter fail to record anything that is interesting. Not only might a new way be found of handling the jottings but just browsing through them can often be rewarding. Sometimes the juxtaposition of two or three apparently unrelated ideas can trigger off an entirely new train of thought.

For my part I carry a small tape recorder on which I record anything of interest. These items are then transferred on to cards which I keep in a file. I even jot down ideas for titles on them. The titles might not have a novel to attach themselves to yet but the day might come. Certainly I've had cause to be grateful for them in the past.

ILLUSTRATION 2: An idea germinates

**Themes can come from anywhere -
out of the air, a conversation overheard or,
as here, from a newspaper cutting.**

The chance find of this type of brief news item
planted the seed of an idea which would eventually grow
into the novel OF MASKS AND MINDS.

Scope for a novel?
Insanity - touchy subject
Genius bordering
on madness?

* with alternating
periods of highly
creative activity

or any man

Sounds a very risky
op. Why would he
submit willingly?
Scared?

Creative people said to
suffer more than most.*
An artist would find
work hard.

Dilemmas?

Family - for or against
Wife - depressives
very hard to live
with. Painful to
observe.

What arguments?
(Check with psychologist/
psychiatrist)

Possible themes
Man's right to control
his mind   Too often done

Wife faced with
decision?
If she op succeeds,
life returns to normal.
If not, he'll hate her.
NO WIN SITUATION!

Job
Mathematical theorist?
Bit abstruse for a book
Artist/writer? - they
have a more public
end product.
Musician? - creating
more powerful music
as mania grips -
that could be destroyed
by op?

If he loses his
reasoning or ability
to create will he
be aware of it?
Vegetating could destroy
him - especially if
work is more important
than life.

Could he
come to terms
with it?

Brain operation restores sanity

A REVOLUTIONARY brain operation holds out the promise of relief to patients lapsing into previously untreatable forms of severe clinical depression.

The operation, called a prefrontal leucotomy is being increasingly used by surgeons as a treatment for intractable mental disorders where sufferers would probably decline into insanity. The leucotomy consists of surgical interruption of one or more nerve tracts in the frontal lobe of the brain.

Whilst early results have proved favourable, side and after effects have raised doubts in some quarters of the medical profession as to its use in general cases.

The argument surrounding the case of Professor X, an eminent mathematical theorist, has demonstrated the dilemma facing surgeons. The operation, whilst fully expected to halt the steady worsening of his mind's condition, could leave him lethargic and unable to continue normal working life.

A London psycho-neurologist says the risk is that the patient may regain his sanity, but with diminished ability to pursue routine activities, possible permanent memory loss, and reasoning impairment. It is a sad fact that brilliant minds, such as the Professor's, could be lost to the scientific world as a result.

15

3 Marrying Theme and Plot

Continuing with the assumption that a writer has a strong theme but wants a plot that will bring out the best of it in the novel, are there any specific plotting rules that might guide him?

The writer must remember first of all that his primary role in the novel is to entertain his reader. The good story-teller will always do this by inserting moments of humour or nail biting episodes that develop the conflict within the story as well as moving it along. The novel can't be all black and white, or on the same emotional level, or the reader will become justifiably bored.

The plot of any work of fiction has also to engage the reader's emotions. The choice of these emotions (because there can be more than one involved) should have a direct relationship to the theme. A novel about a totalitarian regime would show sympathy for its victims and, in all likelihood, dislike for their oppressors. A novel about a mother's concern for her child would evoke love and understanding. A novel about war might involve aggression, pathos, grief, and so on. Once the choice or choices are made, the resolution of conflicts should further strengthen the emotional elements.

Yet in spite of all the advice they get, many novices still find plotting very difficult. What are the most important factors for them to bear in mind whilst working out their story-lines?

Remember the suspense and conflict elements. These should be built into the plot so that tension builds up from chapter to chapter. This applies as much to a straight novel as to a thriller. All books, no matter what their theme or content, should have conflict and suspense as two of their main ingredients. They are such important factors that perhaps we ought to deal with them at greater length later on.

The plot structure can be thought of in terms of a rising graph. Inevitably the theme has some bearing on the shape - a thriller usually has a higher starting point than a straight novel - but even with thrillers I prefer a fairly muted beginning, one that suggests mystery and action to come rather than an action scene itself. Then a slow build-up of tension, with an occasional mini-crisis on the way, to the final climax.

Then you're not in favour of novels that start in the middle of some strong action, and keep it 'on the boil'?

No, because a reader is capable of only so much emotion and if you give him a surfeit of heavy scenes early in the book, there is a real danger that he'll be sated when he reaches the climax. There is also the technical side to consider. A plot structure should resemble an escarpment, a steady slope on one side to a high peak, then a steep drop. This is because in general the denouement of a novel should never take more than a few pages or it can become an anticlimax. If we begin our novel with a Himalayan peak, how do we find ones that are even higher for our mini-crises and our climax?

What are these mini-crises you speak of? Can you give an example from your work?

They may be likened to early tremors before an earthquake, and can range from quarrels between the major characters to sub-plots within the main story-line. In 633 SQUADRON I had a pilot so furious with his navigator for sleeping with his girl friend that, to punish him, he broke orders and attacked a German flak ship. This ship radioed back for fighter help and as a consequence heavy casualties were suffered when the full squadron, taking the same flight path, flew out on its main mission of the day. These casualties in turn affected all that was to happen later. In this way a sub-plot can provide an additional crisis within a story and yet help sweep the main plot along to its final climax.

Your novel OF MASKS AND MINDS is one in which conflict of many kinds played a key role. How did you set about structuring it into a novel?

By posing doubts, conflicts, and mystery. But first I felt I must turn the scientist into a famous musical composer because, rightly or wrongly, people believe artists are more dedicated to their work than other men. Then I must have him married to the right kind of woman. She must have the perception to know that, were he able to make the decision himself, he would prefer to continue writing music until his mind snapped irreversibly, rather than become normal again but artistically impotent. With those preliminary elements, the possibilities excited me.

The next step was to pose questions. What would the wife do when confronted by these circumstances? She desperately wants to save her husband's reason but, knowing what music means to him, she will agonise over the operation and keep postponing it. What will make things even worse for her? Surely a mother-in-law who demands the operation. Then let us suppose the wife learns that her husband's condition is due to some hidden guilt and she might yet save both his mind and his music if she can discover the nature of that guilt. But is there time to make this discovery? And does his guilt involve anyone else in the family?

Notice how it is all conflict. Conflict in the woman's mind over her correct decision; conflict with his mother; conflict with his doctor as she delays putting off the operation. And suspense as every delayed day adds to the risk of total madness. Conflict, conflict, conflict, suspense, suspense, suspense. Along with strong and believable characters, these are vital ingredients in the structuring of a novel.

This questioning process could go on indefinitely and lead down many blind alleys. How can a writer identify that point at which to stop the exploration and start the writing?

The trick, of course, is to squeeze every drop of drama from an idea without overdoing it. It is a difficult process because, as with most good ideas, there are literally hundreds of possible permutations, and a writer wants to choose the best that he can. He'll never get the absolute best, of course, but he should persevere until he begins to tire of the idea. That is a warning sign to stop and to extract the most promising plot from the wealth of options.

Of course, it goes without saying that, while constructing his plot, the writer must have invented plausible and living characters to enact its dramatic situations, otherwise all their power will be lost. But because of their importance to the novel, characters and the way they are created should be discussed separately.

A word of warning here. A writer should think very carefully about his story-line as he constructs his plot. Not all ideas that at first seem promising lend themselves to a full length novel and it is better to find this out at this stage than when one is halfway through the novel itself.

Is it at this point that the writer should determine whether the emphasis will be on the events of the story, with characterisation unaffected, or in the growth of characters, with events having a lesser significance?

I have reservations here, which perhaps we might discuss later, but I follow your question. It is true that in much popular fiction the accent is on events rather than characterisation. In other words, the chosen characters play out the part the author has selected for them and come out at the end the same people they were in the beginning: there is no development of character. Examples of these books are everywhere in the form of thrillers, detective stories, romantic stories, and similar works of light fiction.

In general it is in the stronger and more significant novel that characters dominate or influence the story-line, just as in real life a man's character and behaviour affects his life and the people around him. A development of character, for better or worse, is also often seen in these novels. These works are more difficult to write because they not only require their author to have an understanding of human nature, but they also require considerable skill to portray that understanding in the characters he creates.

If a writer feels he is only equipped to use one or the other of these formulae, then perhaps this is the time to make his choice.

Working on a more subtle level within the plot, a good writer can also introduce the deeper implications of his theme, if he feels that theme is strong enough to influence the reader's prejudices. Your novels do this very successfully. What is the secret?

For me, the most important rule is never to overplay your hand. Remember that argument on a conscious level seldom changes a prejudiced mind. Seeing it coming, the opponent is ready and quick to counterattack. No, we novelists have to be more cunning than that. Unlike the brave and foolish who launch their attacks against the well-defended front gates, we sneak round the back and creep in through unguarded windows. We know the mind can be controlled, but not the heart. So we create our story in such a way that the enemy is deceived. To change our metaphors, we lead him along a path of interest and entertainment and present him with characters who at times seem to justify his prejudice. Only when he is in sympathy with the characters we are using as bait, do we suddenly jerk on the line and hook him. Then he is left staring at the tragedy that his prejudices have wrought.

This might not change his views immediately, but we have broken into his mind and planted a seed that hopefully might grow and aid him to develop a new philosophy.

Did you deliberately set out to do this in your anti-apartheid novel, LAWS BE THEIR ENEMY? I'm thinking of Dr Morkel, the Afrikaans doctor who, although a believer in apartheid, still provides charity for the coloured children in his district.

You're quite right. Having lived in South Africa, I had learned how easy it is for otherwise decent men to accept a flawed political policy if exposed to it from birth. By using such men as examples in a drama, one can hopefully create an influence without provoking an aggressive counter response.

The subtle changing of character seems to be a technique you like using. I'm thinking again of books like THE TORMENTED and THE WAR GOD.

Yes, but the methods used differ in accordance with the story. In these two books it was the corroding effect of violence that changed the views and beliefs of some of the characters.

CLASSICS v PULP

Writers are advised to 'study the classics' as a learning process. Would you agree with that practice as an aid to plot development?

I agree that beginners ought to study the work of classical novelists. But at the same time they shouldn't listen to the literary snobs who advise them to research nothing else. The classics are excellent for studying characterisation because it is generally accepted that the study and development of character, rather than plot, is the basis of true literature and the more talented the author, the more he invents characters that live. But the reverse is true of the less talented writer. Because he finds characterisation difficult, he has to compensate by learning how to tell a good story, and in this field he often excels.

In other words he has to substitute craft for art. A very high percentage of popular novelists come into this category and their sales suggest the public at large prefers their product. They, the authors, won't be remembered in posterity, of course, because in general it is well-drawn characters, and not plots, that are remembered - Hamlet, Othello, King Lear, down to Rhett Butler and Scarlett O'Hara come to mind - but while their books are being published, the less talented writers are often the ones who are better known and the more successful financially.

To me, however, the ideal novel is the one that marries art and craft i.e. has vivid, life-like characters involved in an exciting, well-told story. Events should have their effect on characters and characters should create or at least have their effect on events, as they do in real life.

This is why I had reservations about a writer choosing one or the other formula. I would like him to get into the habit of interlacing characters and events from the onset, although I accept he will find it easier initially to use the lighter fiction formula.

Whatever his ambitions, however, he can only gain by studying both the classics and popular fiction. Provided he has talent and the other necessary attributes, a mastery of the two formulae ought to make him a complete novelist.

ILLUSTRATION 3: The plot takes shape

An idea is one thing, but can it make a novel?
Plotting a chart of the likely events and traumas, clarifies the thought processes.

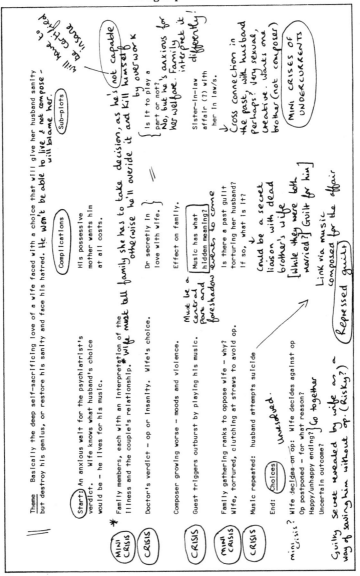

4 Characters

*We've already mentioned the importance of creating living charac-
ters within the novel. In that act of creation, the novelist has the
chance to play God and breathe life into his cast. If the novel is to
have the maximum credibility, what is the best approach?*

The task is to create characters whose natures will allow them to
play out the roles the plot has given them. As every story and its
nuances are different, it follows that every character should be
different, just as they are in life. In other words our characters
should be as nearly as possible suited to their roles.

I can't emphasise enough the importance of good casting here. In
real life there are certain things some people will do and others will
not do. Some men and women could never commit murder: some
men and women could never commit adultery. Others are capable
of both. A good plot is ruined by shallow and implausible characters and readers will sense that lack of characterisation, even if they
are not sure why they have found the book unsatisfying.

This does not mean the characters cannot develop within the story.
Indeed they should. We all learn something every day of our lives
and so should our characters. This applies particularly if the novel
stretches over a long time span.

*The major weakness I find with new students is in using family and
friends as a basis for their characterisation. Consequently they are
then inhibited by rigid adherence to those personae, and create
major problems for themselves. Should they always invent characters?*

I think so. I don't think it wise to use real people unless it is one's
specific intention. We seldom really know people, even those very
close to us. (Do we even know ourselves?) This mistaken confidence in our knowledge can produce at worst characters that seem
strangely out of focus and at best cause immense problems before
one gets them right.

I believe another reason that causes problems is our knowledge of
what has happened to these people in their real lives. It is as if this
knowledge has cut a groove in our mind and the moment we try to

make them do something different in the story, our mind slips back into this groove like a needle on a scratched record.

Of course the process of creating characters is a mysterious thing and perhaps we all do use some aspects of people we know. But I don't believe it should be done consciously. There is also the problem of libel here. Writers should create characters to fit their story-lines as inventively as they can and try to keep people they know well out of mind.

I don't believe any writer knows with certainty how he creates his characters. Undoubtedly something of himself is in them all. As I have said, writers are very often complex people with many facets to their personalities and some of these facets can be seen in the characters they create - a sobering thought when one creates a particularly nasty villain! Other facets are probably drawn subconsciously from the many hundreds or even thousands of people one has known. One can theorise for a long time on this but it remains a mysterious process.

You have just said a writer should not base characters on people he knows very well. Yet wasn't your recently completed Yorkshire trilogy based, even if loosely, on your own family?

Yes, it was. Perhaps that is why I'm advising beginners not to make the same mistake. When the trilogy was commissioned, I felt, like so many others before me, that it would be a relatively easy task with so much background knowledge already on hand.

It proved entirely the reverse. In fact, it wasn't until a friend reminded me to look upon my parents and their lives as totally fictional elements that the books began to move forward.

Nevertheless there are times when one can use well known characters with safety. I am thinking about novels based on some charismatic character who might fascinate the novelist, such as Joan of Arc, Rupert Brooke, or Winston Churchill. I did this myself when I wrote about Napoleon and Wellington in my book WATERLOO and because they are long dead and I had not known them in the flesh, there was no inhibiting effect.

With deceased people, there is also no problem of libel, although in my view one should keep as close to the known facts of their lives as possible. If they are alive, however, and you wish to include them in a novel, then it is wise to ask their permission. On the other hand, if your intention is not to write about them directly but to create a character based on them, then tread very warily because even if your book states clearly that its characters are not meant to depict any living person, a clever lawyer can soon make this assertion look very fragile. Nevertheless it is another way of designing a plot and can be talked about in more detail later.

Genre books so often rely on stereotyped characters - the so-called trio of the good, the bad and the ugly. Would you agree that successful novels draw rounded characters, and that this fuller characterisation should be encouraged?

Genre novels do often use stereotyped characters. They are written for a public who want easy reading and clichés of character are as easy to identify as clichés of situation and language. These books often sell very well, so we must define what successful means. If we are not talking about sales but only about quality, then it is indisputable that characters should never be presented in black and white terms. No one is perfect and no one is entirely bad. Indeed, just as humour needs a touch of sadness to highlight it, so good and evil need their converse.

I remember very vividly a story the famous Norwegian poet Zinken Hopp once told me. During the war she lived in a block of flats in Bergen opposite the National Theatre where the Gestapo interrogated their prisoners. The Commandant, whom she said looked like the Michelin man (all tyres of flesh), had taken the flat next to her own and sometimes she met him in the lift. Although she knew he was daily ordering the torture of her fellow countrymen, she felt no fear of him. He and the whole scene seemed larger than life and too bizarre to take in.

Then, one evening, there was a knock on her door and she found the Commandant standing there with a white kitten in his arms. Saluting her politely, as he always did, he told her he had found it in his flat and was worried because it would not drink the milk he gave it. Would she be so kind as to take care of it as he would not want it to suffer or die? From that moment on, Zinken said, her legs trembled every time she saw him. The lesson, of course, is that light emphasises darkness and vice versa.

A word of warning about the characters we invent. All of us without exception have our pet dislikes of certain types of person and it is a great temptation to use them as our villains or at least as the less savoury characters in our stories. There is nothing wrong with doing this once or twice but if we continue with our prejudice it will begin to show.

You mean there is a danger that a writer might give his villains the same characteristics in all his novels?

If a writer lets his prejudices run away with him, yes.

I'm interested in your choice of the word prejudice. Are you saying that if writers are to represent the full spectrum of the human character they must have a special kind of tolerance for the frailties of human nature?

Tolerance might be too embracing a word. I would prefer understanding or in some cases sympathy. Without these attributes, a writer might forget he should not create black and white characters and overload his villains with faults. That is the danger of using characters he particularly dislikes.

Ironically, however, there is a certain therapy in writing about one's prejudices in this way. To write about any character, a writer needs to know him very well and this means building up a kind of dossier on him before the writing begins. The writer won't use much of this dossier but as it should go back to the character's early life, his family, and environment, it will also include the reasons why he has turned out the pleasant or unpleasant person he is. As to know is often to understand, it follows that writing about people one dislikes can often change one's mind even to the point of feeling sympathy for them. This is one of the least talked about aspects of writing and yet in my view one of the most important. It teaches one tolerance and that tolerance remains whether one's books are published or not. Perhaps that explains why a gathering of writers, beginners and successful ones alike, can often be a pleasant experience!

There are dangers, then, in using family and friends in novels, but what of one's own life and experiences?

I believe one should use one's personal experiences as sparingly as possible. There are two good reasons for this. If you write too much about yourself in a book, it is in danger of containing too much fact and that not only restricts the freedom of plot construction but also has a curiously deadening effect on the story-line. You are too close to yourself to make yourself seem real. I know this sounds ridiculous but it is true.

The second danger of using one's own life in excess is of running out of material for subsequent books. All writers use personal experience to underline certain incidents because this can make them graphic, but however exciting and full a writer's life is or has been - and a sensible one keeps adding to his experiences - even the richest bank balance is in danger of running dry if plundered too often. This so often happens to novelists who make a big killing and then retire to an ivory castle where nothing more happens to them. Ten years later they wonder why their books are no longer selling. Life has moved on while they have remained stationary using up the last of their memories and experiences.

Better by far to create imaginary characters and incidents and intermingle one's personal experiences sparingly. Otherwise one's later books can be a grave disappointment to author and publisher alike. Many years ago, when visiting a Dutch publisher who was about to publish my first novel, he confronted me with a very well-known novel by another English writer and asked me if I would publish it if I were in his shoes.

Surprised by the question, I told him of the success it had been in England. He said he knew all about that but he took on authors for their future promise and he didn't feel that this man, by using up so much of his life in his first book, would produce anything as good again. Sadly, I think he was proven right.

Having created characters, how much visual description should a beginner give them in the text?

I believe as little as the story needs. Every man and every woman has his or her fantasy counterpart. It follows therefore that if a writer can suggest to them an image of that fantasy person, he will greatly increase their enjoyment of his story. He can't do this positively, of course, but he can do it by offering a kind of skeleton of the character which the reader will then flesh out himself.

Isn't there a danger in being so sparse with details that the reader will be left with cardboard characters?

I'm not suggesting one should take this advice too literally. If a man is tall, it should be stated because his height might have a bearing on the story-line. Equally a girl's beauty will have to be mentioned because it will give her life advantages and disadvantages denied to a plainer girl. I was referring more to the subtler aspects of appearance, the tip-turned nose, the dimpled cheek, the winsome smile, etc, *unless* these attributes have a bearing on the story itself. If they do not, then I believe it is more effective to leave the reader to flesh out such details himself. As I've suggested, by unconsciously creating his fantasy heroine he will follow her progress with much more interest than if she were just another woman.

Of course this doesn't mean a writer should leave his characters' actions and speech to the reader's imagination because the story-line (and the reader's fantasies) depend on them. In the same way that characters should never be allowed to do things that their temperaments forbid, they should never say things unsuited to their personalities. The words they use ought to be as individual as their fingerprints, yet how often do we read novels in which one could shift expressions from the mouths of one character to another's without any notable difference? These are the truly cardboard characters. Although this kind of poor and stilted dialogue is more often related to thrillers, romances, and their like, it can be seen in any kind of novel and should be avoided like the plague.

Having said this, I'm fully aware that dialogue is difficult to some writers but its proper use must be learned because it is the main medium of communication between people and up to 50 per cent of a novel might consist of it. But perhaps we should discuss dialogue more fully in due course.

A common expression is 'the characters ran away with me'. Can or should this happen?

This is a remark I keep on hearing and it really is an amateurish one. How can characters run away? They are the writer's creation, specifically designed to do as he tells them. If he can't control his characters it means a number of things and none of them to his credit. It means either he has an undisciplined mind and cannot keep it on the track he has set himself, or that he has created the wrong characters for his story-line. Or, alternatively, that he has the wrong story-line for them, for a story can be changed after the writing has commenced, just as a character can be changed.

None of this means, as some people like to think, that the writer has created characters so powerful they have become creatures in their own right. They may become that if he has given them a good story-line but certainly not if he allows them to charge about all over the countryside doing their own thing. The writer is their master. He plays God by creating them but he does not, after giving them their share of right and wrong, stand back and let them make the same mess of the world that we humans are making. Art is an improvement on Nature (or so we like to think) and in our make-believe world our characters move sometimes quietly, sometimes passionately, but always inevitably towards the destiny we have planned for them.

What is the writer to do who has a fully developed story-line or synopsis, but for some reason simply can't 'see' his characters?

This happens more often than some people think: indeed it probably happens to all novelists at one time or another. It has certainly happened to me. When it does, my method is to begin the novel and keep on writing until I find the characters starting to come to life. Oddly enough, when they do they often seem more suited to the story than others created in a more traditional way.

Not every writer will agree with me here, but I would ask that the point be considered. There is no doubt that a novel is ruined when its characters are not properly designed for their roles but instead are made to obey the demands of the plot willy nilly. Then doesn't it make some sense to suggest that if the characters grow while one writes the book, they should be perfectly suited for their roles because in one sense their roles have created them?

In some respects this resembles the way one sometimes only discovers the theme of a novel when halfway through writing it. As with that discovery, it might mean re-writing a few early chapters when the characters were still in embryo, so to speak, but it is more than worthwhile if the book is improved by the alterations.

This isn't a method many writers will recommend and I've only used it myself very occasionally. Nevertheless I've found it works for me. Always remember writing is an art, not a science, and there are many ways of reaching the same goal.

NAMES

Are names important to the content and form of the novel, or will any old name do? I notice that in most of your novels you tend to use simpler, everyday names. Is that intentional on your part?

Yes, it is. I shy from glamorous names because they can give an artificial quality to a man or woman and so detract from their substance and their integrity. Also, in the main they tend to be fashionable and that can give an ephemeral quality to a theme that might be timeless.

At the same time, names are important. Just as a writer should make characters as different in appearance and speech as possible, so he should use names that can't be confused with one another. Confusion occurs when names begin with the same consonant or vowel, a thing that should always be avoided. Family names can be obtained from a number of sources. For modern names there is no easier one than the current telephone directory. For regional names, old records and gravestones in local cemeteries are first class sources. First names can be a little more difficult to invent, although it is possible to obtain books that give exhaustive lists of the forenames of both sexes.

Where one has to be careful is to pick names that are, or were, popular in the time-scale of the novel one is writing. If a novel is set in the present, a list of modern forenames should be made for its younger characters but they should not be too glamorous unless they are designed for actors and their like. Too many Crystals and Alexes can sound very corny or amateurish.

ILLUSTRATION 4: A story needs people

The characters must be different, in types and attitudes if the novel is to maintain interest for a reader.

The author needs to know his cast as well as he knows his own family - before he puts pen to paper.

Theme: Love and guilt. A wife's sacrifice.

Who do I need?	Description	Characteristics	Names?
Wife *Tall, dark hair grey eyes*	30ish Relatively ordinary. Composed *Nerves torn by decision*	Inner strength Doesn't shirk hard things.	~~Joan~~ Jean (Mary) ~~Margaret~~
Husband	35+? Highly strung, Guilt ridden *Brooding* *Piercing(mad?)eyes Wiry*	Artistic genius Temper and bouts of depression	Richard ~~Henry~~ *pompous* (James) Peter
(Family)Mother	60s/70s Ferocious and domineering *Patricia Straight back!*	Obsessed by her children. Little artistic recognition	Charlotte Edith
Sister	40 Thin, vinegary (Olive Oyl?)	Waspish and jealous Repressed (by her mother. ~~Un~~Married	~~Freda~~ *not Minnie acid enough*
Brother	Late 30s Eager, Wounded in war	A sense of honour In love with his sister-in-law	Frank ~~James~~ *brother's name*
Sister-in-law	30s Lively, A Titian beauty *Glittery, but brittle*	Sexy and knows it Flippancy disguises uncertainty (& guilt?)	~~Diana~~ *Stella!!!*
Half sister *to Diana Stella*	40s Fading looks Tetchy	Frightened of losing looks & husband	Gwyneth *Shorten to Gwen (Welsh?)*
Her husband *? Flash Harry!*	45+ Thick set ageing *Self made self important*	Unhappy at home, is dazzled by Diana	~~Maurice~~ Melvyn *(Welsh too?)*
Doctor	35ish 45ish Neat 'country tweed' *Average build*	Love for wife - but hides it	John
~~Psychiatrist~~	~~50s, professional~~	~~Professionalism~~ *not really needed*	

Mother *(widow)*

Mary = ~~Richard~~ James   Frank   ~~Freda~~ Minnie Ethel   David = Stella *half sister*
                                                                    Gwen = ~~Maurice~~ Mervyn

Family name? Needs to be middle-class, English.

Portland   Charlton   Henderson   ~~McAllister~~   Brightwell

5   The Setting

We haven't mentioned the setting of the proposed novel yet. Would you determine its location at this point before a synopsis is written?

Yes, but unless the plot depends on the location, the setting needs only be sketched in at this stage and not developed.

What advice would you give a beginner here? Play safe and choose a location he already knows well?

Yes. If his plot depends on human emotions, which are basic to all men, it can feasibly be set almost anywhere, provided these emotions are not dependent on elements exclusive to one particular country. If they are not, he should always opt for his own country: he knows it better than foreign lands. It is only when topographical, cultural or religious factors affect the story that one might need a foreign setting.

At the same time certain plots can be improved by dramatic or glamorous backdrops but if a writer chooses a story of this nature, he should do his homework well. Successful books have been written about places the author has never visited but a great deal of care has to be taken over the selection of details.

But, as I say, such details are rarely required for the synopsis. It is only when the novel is being written from the synopsis that their need becomes apparent.

RESEARCH

If a novel is to be set in a foreign location, detailed research will be a necessary element. Are you saying it isn't necessary to do it while the novel is in the gestation stage?

That's correct. But it is a mistake many a novice writer makes. Unless he has money to squander, he shouldn't go to his chosen country when he is writing his synopsis. He should wait until he has written the first draft of his novel. This might sound double Dutch but if he goes beforehand, he will have no way of knowing what information he needs.

This is because in drawing up a synopsis a writer can't know what details the final novel will demand. He will come back, as I once did before writing a thriller set in the Arctic, with notebooks full of information, only to discover they contain hardly any of the details he needs when his story-line is expanded into the novel. In my case this meant going all the way back to the Arctic - a most expensive business and a mistake I've never made again.

But is it possible to write the story, if only in first draft form, without being able to paint in the background?

In fact it is fairly easy. One leaves gaps in the story-line where the foreign material is needed and then fills them in after one's return. After all one is seldom writing detailed descriptions about a country. In modern novels such descriptions are becoming less and less necessary. Extensive public travel is one reason and a second is television which shows viewers in technicolour what foreign countries are like.

You are saying these factors free novelists from detailed descriptive passages?

Unless the book depends a great deal on detail, yes. Usually only snatches of description are necessary. But if a book should need more details, or if one feels, as I do, that it gains a subtle verisimilitude from its author having experienced a country's sights and sounds, then how much more sensible to go there after the first draft is written when one knows exactly what is needed. Usually the copy can then be obtained in a day or two.

For the writer able to afford foreign travel, this is what I would advise. Books and TV programmes are very good at preparing the reader for abbreviated descriptions, but for a writer, a visit to the country not only gives his novel an authority that might otherwise be lacking but might in itself trigger off new ideas. He might also see sights, like vultures perched on acacia trees, that he can use to heighten the drama of his story.

A further, if obvious advantage, is that a visit does help avoid those ghastly errors that can be so easily made if one is only using reference books for copy. It's a sad but true fact that while readers seldom write and tell you they like your book, they just love to write about any errors they find.

Even so, foreign visits can have their drawbacks. Far too many writers, who have fallen in love with a country on a recent visit, lace their next novel with descriptions that might bring pleasure to them but only bring a yawn to their readers. It's all too easy to make the book sound like a travelogue. Descriptions should never appear for their own sake but only if their appearance is a necessary ingredient in the story.

Nevertheless, I find many new novelists do use exotic settings as if they feel these are necessary or a passport to their success.

It often happens with writers who, perhaps subconsciously, have no confidence in their story-line and so hope to disguise its weakness by a glamorous backdrop. In a way it is similar to the writers who use explicit sex scenes every ten or so pages in an effort to keep a reader turning the pages over on a poorly-written story. If foreign settings are unnecessary for a plot I would never use them. As I said earlier, when it comes to emotion, people are much the same the world over. So why make things more difficult for oneself if a story sits as well in Britain as anywhere else? A scene in Cornwall with a black cloud brooding over a tor can be just as menacing in its effect as any scene abroad.

At the same time, you did just say that foreign travel might trigger off new ideas. Has this happened to you?

Quite often. New customs, new faces, new sights and sounds: they are all grist to the mill if one has the kind of mind that can weave them into a story. At the same time, if a writer is looking for the details of a story already written, he has to be disciplined enough to store these ideas away for future novels.

For me, my richest ideas have come when I've been taking a simple holiday abroad. I put this down to the way I travel. If on my own, I never set myself an itinerary of any kind. Instead I go to the country of my choosing and there just 'follow my nose'. Time and again when I've done this I've had some worthwhile or exciting experience. It is almost as if the refusal to plan one's life allows fate to come up with the experience it wishes one to have.

Perhaps a good simile would be a man getting into a rowing boat. He rows out to the centre of the stream and then ships his oars. This allows the current to take hold of him and his boat and take them where it wills.

If one were philosophical about it, one could perhaps argue that by planning our lives too fully we never achieve our true destiny. We bypass the natural signposts of our lives. But if we relinquish control, those signposts come to us in natural sequence. Certainly I have had some extraordinary experiences by following my nose in this way and they have given me more than one novel.

Can you give any examples of how such experiences have provided material for your novels?

My novel THE DEVIL BEHIND ME came this way. I was drifting through Sweden when I came across a man and a girl who were being hunted by a particularly unpleasant criminal and his gang. Some years earlier, the couple told me, they had 'shopped' this gangster and now that he was out of prison he was determined to take his revenge on them. To save themselves, the couple had to reach Stockholm where there was a witness who could effect a retrial of the gangster and have him imprisoned again.

A little sceptical about their story, I nevertheless offered to take them to Stockholm in my car. On the way my doubts disappeared when I discovered a car was trailing us. By turning off the main road, we managed to evade it, and as it was now ahead of us on the Stockholm road, we thought we were safe.

However, we had all forgotten that one has to cross bridges to enter Stockholm, and all the gangsters needed to do was put a man on each bridge to pick us up again. So we had one or two hairy moments before we were fortunate enough to find the witness and the couple were safe.

I had another absurd experience a few days later. Hearing that Swedish Lapland was a wonderland of colour in the early autumn, I took a train to Kiruna. From there I made my way to the Abisko National Park. While out walking one day in only shirt and shorts, for although the nights were icy, the days were warm, I lost my way. This meant that to catch the only train back to Abisko, I had to run ten kilometres along the track to catch it or I would be stranded for the night in totally inadequate clothing.

What I didn't know when I set off was that the railway track ran through tunnel after tunnel, all of which seemed cut to take only a single train. Moreover, some were over half a mile in length and I could find no safety alcoves for a man to take refuge in. But it was only after I had stumbled in pitch darkness through a couple of them and was deep into a third that I realised the extent of my danger. I knew that huge iron ore trains ran from Kiruna to Narvik every hour and as none had passed me since I found the track, one must be due at any time.

So I ran and ran in the pitch darkness, bruising myself against the rocky walls and thinking I heard a train pounding behind me every time I paused for breath. When I finally stumbled out of that tunnel and a massive freight train thundered past me, I estimated I had escaped death by no more than ten seconds.

But what a story I had! Until then I had already worked out ways I could use the man and the girl in a thriller, but as yet hadn't thought of a dramatic ending. Now the tunnel incident had provided me with exactly what I wanted.

I returned home two weeks later with almost a complete novel in my head. I wrote it in six months and it sold in Britain, in Europe, and in America. I also sold the film rights. All because I had made no plans for my holiday but simply 'followed my nose'.

Didn't your anti-apartheid novel, LAWS BE THEIR ENEMY, have similar beginnings?

In some ways it had. I was living in South Africa the year the apartheid laws were passed and realising their implications I did some research on their effects. As the blacks were the ones to suffer, I decided after a while to disguise myself as one. I dyed my hair and skin and wore a pair of overalls and dark glasses to hide my blue eyes. As I could not speak Afrikaans, a coloured youth from the firm where I was working very courageously offered to go around with me.

I'd no plan in mind. I thought I would just wander around in my disguise and see what happened. But after a while we found ourselves in District Six, the notorious area of Cape Town where even the police seldom went. There I began to see some graphic examples of the resentment the blacks were feeling towards the new laws and with my interest aroused, we kept going back night after night.

Our luck ran out on the fifth night. We were in a drinking house frequented by extremists when someone saw through my disguise and six criminals armed with knives chased us through the backstreets. From what we had witnessed that night, there was no doubt they intended to close our mouths by killing us. However, we managed to escape, and although it wasn't an experience I'd like again, it provided me with just the kind of material I needed for the book.

You have visited every country in which you've set a book - with one exception. THE TORMENTED doesn't take place in a real country, and yet it has a great sense of reality and is possibly the most powerful of your novels. Didn't its location pose special problems of its own?

Yes. For all kinds of thematic reasons it had to be set in South America but because of personal problems I could not go there at the time I was writing it.

My solution was to create a fictitious country within the continent. By using that method I could not be criticised if 'my' country contained some landmark or peculiarity not present elsewhere, although even then I had to be careful that its climate and topography matched in every way the countries on its borders.

How long did it take you to design this 'new' country?

Four months in all. I was quite pleased with the result although the amount of work necessary to avoid mistakes was intimidating. For that reason, if a writer can manage it, it is far better to visit his chosen country with a notebook or tape recorder and take in its sights, smells, and sounds in person.

Sights, sounds and smells! Should a writer try to evoke all five senses in his work?

He should when he writes the final draft of his novel. Every sense of the reader should be stimulated to make him feel he is living and breathing in the novel's setting.

So far we've defined setting only as the country in which a book is based. But it can also apply to the everyday whereabouts of characters, such as their workplace or leisure activities. Is it necessary to have detailed knowledge of unusual jobs and procedures, or can it be glossed over?

Again it depends on the story-line. If detailed descriptions are necessary, a writer should keep as much as possible to work places or activities that he is familiar with. If he must include settings or activities of which he knows nothing, then he should try to arrange visits to them. Unless he is writing about military or State secrets, this is usually possible. One of the attractive things about being a writer is that most people are only too happy to take one round their place of work and explain their role there.

ILLUSTRATION 5: Finding a locale

Where to place the events of the story is one more vital element in the overall design.

Fine details are not required at this early stage but being prepared will point the way to necessary research.

The action is to take place in a home, over a series of days. The family are to be essentially English, middle-class. Is there any advantage in setting it abroad?

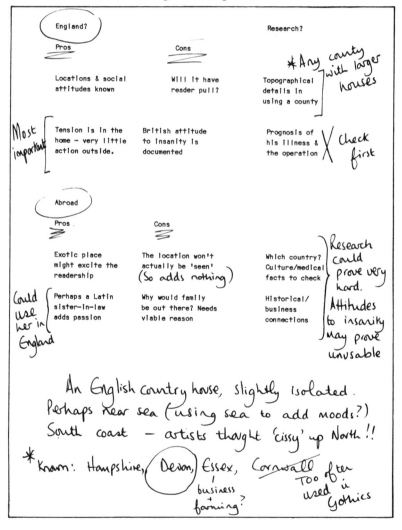

England?

Research?

Pros

Cons

* Any county with larger houses

Locations & social attitudes known

Will it have reader pull?

Topographical details in using a county

Most important

Tension is in the home – very little action outside.

British attitude to insanity is documented

Prognosis of his illness & the operation

Check first

Abroad

Pros

Cons

Exotic place might excite the readership

The location won't actually be 'seen' (So adds nothing)

Which country? Culture/medical facts to check

Research could prove very hard.

Could use her in England

Perhaps a Latin sister-in-law adds passion

Why would family be out there? Needs viable reason

Historical/business connections

Attitudes to insanity may prove unusable

An English country house, slightly isolated.
Perhaps near sea (using sea to add moods?)
South coast – artists thought 'cissy' up North !!

* Known: Hampshire, (Devon,) Essex, Cornwall often
business + farming?
Too often used in Gothics

6 Synopsis

Now that ideas, themes, plots, characters, and settings have been considered, I take it a novice writer would be ready to construct a synopsis. However, it's a word that seems to make many novices flinch. In the context of a novel, it's a detailed fleshing of the plot, but is it vital, or even necessary, to construct a synopsis?

It isn't absolutely necessary if a writer has a marvellous memory but it is a great help to the rest of us. Its main purpose is to aid a writer to get from A to Z and this can be done either as a continuous precis of the entire story, or as a series of events split up into chapters. I use the latter method myself, though it's a matter of individual preference. The synopsis is a blueprint for my own guidance, and it gives me a rough guide as to how long the book is likely to be. But either method can be used satisfactorily.

From what you've already said, I take it your blueprint would cover only the broad outline of the story?

It is unlikely that one of mine would show too much detail. Although I've talked at some length about structuring an idea, I personally don't use very detailed synopses.

The reason is because the really creative part of writing is in the writing itself. People will come to you and give you an idea with a smugness that as good as says: "You see. I could be a writer too if I had the time." They truly believe it, and doesn't it irritate?

The truth is they wouldn't have a clue what to do with the idea if asked to make a novel of it. The planning of a synopsis alone would defeat them but even that is more or less a mechanical or constructional task. One considers this possibility and that, one puts one scene in Chapter 10 and then brings it forward to Chapter 8 or whatever. It is very much like assembling a jigsaw. One knows the opening and hopefully one knows the end, but the bits in between have to be assembled correctly to create the maximum effect.

Does this mean that, although you don't use a detailed synopsis yourself, you would recommend a beginner to have one?

Yes, because for one thing, in giving the idea such careful thought, a beginner will eliminate many factors that might otherwise clutter up his novel, and sometimes elimination is as important as creation. My advice is to write a fairly detailed synopsis which is split up into chapters. This will not only help the beginner to fit in his mini-crises but also give him an idea how long his book is going to run. In doing all this, he should pay particular attention to the time factor and try to create characters suited to the roles he is giving them.

Another factor it is important to determine is which person to write the story in. This is because the construction of the novel depends on the viewpoint of the author. I won't go into details here because I'm certain you'll want to talk about viewpoint later but a deter-mination of 1st or 3rd person is necessary at this stage.

It's also important to construct the synopsis so that its hero and heroine appear in the opening paragraphs and the villain not far behind. This will save time later when the novel itself is begun.

At the same time, a writer shouldn't expect to keep to this final synopsis when he begins to write the novel. As I have said, when he reaches that stage, he is entering the truly creative part of the work, and in spite of all the effort he's put into the idea so far, to his surprise he'll still think of better situations and developments. This shouldn't disturb him. Indeed, it is how it should be.

You are saying that although a synopsis is very useful and should be fairly detailed, it need not be strictly adhered to once the creation of the book begins?

It isn't a matter of not needing to be. It is the way the mind works when the actual novel is started. It begins digging at a deeper level and so makes more discoveries. This isn't something to worry about. The care the writer has taken over the novel's elements (as against the way those elements might be used later) will still in the long run save him much time and frustration. In other words the synopsis has achieved its function of being the writer's guideline and it still points the way to his ultimate goal.

You see, the formation of the synopsis is craftsmanship, even an aspect of drama, but it is not yet art. Art is what one does with this material. In one writer's hand it will become lead. In another's it will become gold. That is why it does not matter that there are only a limited number of themes. Writers, like everyone else on earth, are all unique and because of this they will continue to produce from those themes works that are in themselves unique.

The fascinating thing is that they will produce these unique works not only from the same synopsis but even from the same opening line. As they follow the laid down chapters, each will see dif-ferent and sometimes better possibilities and their paths will begin to diverge. In some cases their completed novels will bear little resemblance to the skeleton story they created or were given.

Does this happen all the time?

I can't say all the time, but every good writer I've ever spoken to says it has happened to him or her. However keen they were on their original synopsis, it was planned or written in a different mood to their mood when they began to mould a real body from the skeleton. Mysterious forces now take over, new images arrive, better ideas present themselves, a scene becomes unnecessary (perhaps because of a single word from one of the characters), a new character becomes necessary. We each add the flesh to our skeleton in our different ways.

It has certainly happened to me in every book I have written. This is why, if a writer is lucky enough to get an editor to commission an idea, he should not worry too much if his novel moves away from the synopsis he gave that editor. An editor needs a synopsis to present to his Board members who, after accepting it and agreeing on a sum, promptly forget all about it. A good editor, however, understands that a writer needs space and freedom to develop his original idea (although by the time the novel reaches the editor, he himself might well have forgotten the plot details).

One shouldn't expect an editor to mind, therefore, if you give him a differently constructed book to the one that sold him the idea?

An editor is hardly likely to complain if a writer turns out a superior story to the one he originally sent in, which nearly always is the case. Of course this does not mean a writer should turn a murder story into a romance or vice versa - that could cause considerable problems to Mills and Boon! But different scenes, the introduction or elimination of characters, even a change of purpose (as in my novel THE WAR GOD) will be perfectly acceptable as long as the basic idea is retained. The truth is that a good editor will not think highly of a writer if he keeps exactly to his synopsis. He, the editor, knows that only hacks do that. True writers create as they write and the new paths they discover are nearly always more leafy or exciting than the ones originally envisaged.

To finish this point, a writer shouldn't make the mistake of thinking he will get a higher advance if he produces a better novel this way. His editor's tolerance and understanding does not extend *that* far! But the writer himself will know the difference and, as I've already hinted, in a novelist's life personal satisfaction has often to be weighed against financial rewards.

SUBMITTING IDEAS

Is it safe to send off ideas for consideration by the media? What are your views on this?

There are always risks involved because there is no legal copyright on an idea. This does not suggest for one moment that any editor of repute would steal an idea and give it to one of his recognised authors to handle. Nor would a BBC editor or an editor of the other TV companies. That is neither inferred nor suggested.

What should be pointed out, however, is that an editor cannot be responsible for the ethics of his staff and any institution carries the risk of having one employee whose ideas of right or wrong are fudged. Because of his position, he is likely to know a number of writers and because he is aware there is no copyright on ideas, he might be tempted to ingratiate himself by offering one of them your idea, particularly if the writer is an attractive member of the opposite sex!

It happens. And not only with ideas. I've had two works plagiarised over the years. But mine were completed works, not ideas. When ideas are purloined, plagiarism is less easy to define. A person can read an idea, think how good it is, and then forget all about it. But later, perhaps months or years later, when racking his brain for a new idea, yours comes back into his mind. He doesn't recognise it as yours: he has forgotten all about you. It is his now and he works on it with all the enthusiasm a new idea brings.

This isn't in the same league as plagiarism because it is innocently conceived. Yet if the originator hasn't used the idea yet, the effect can be equally damaging.

This warning does not apply only to the staff of publishers and agents. It equally applies to writers. We have just as many doubtful characters in our ranks as any other profession, and I've known authors quite unashamedly steal someone else's idea, usually under the comforting pretext that 'he's only an amateur and couldn't do it the same justice as I will.'

How does one get round this problem? One can't get a publisher interested in an idea without first showing it to him?

It is difficult, I admit, particularly for the beginner who is less likely to have an agent or other friends in the profession as witnesses to his idea. One tip I was given, although one can hardly warn an editor that the precaution has been taken, is to post a duplicate copy of the idea to the writer's bank where it should be kept. If the need ever came, he could then prove by its postmark that it was sent there on the same day that he submitted the idea.

Another way is to print 'private and confidential' on the top of each page of one's idea or script. I have been told by a lawyer this does to some extent cover one against plagiarism.

None of this is any help, however, in preventing a perfectly honest person remembering one's idea later and believing it to be his own. So perhaps the only useful advice I can give here is to be wary. Remember there are as many unscrupulous characters within the writing profession as outside it, and so when a writer gets a good idea, he should talk about it only to his closest friends and even then warn them it is in the strictest confidence.

TIME TO START WRITING?

Assuming a novice is now able to construct a synopsis with the elements we have discussed, what is your advice? To begin writing the novel itself and introduce the other necessary ingredients, such as viewpoint, suspense, etc, as he writes or should he consider them first?

An experienced novelist would probably begin the novel now because these additional elements will come naturally to him as he writes. But the novice would be wise to consider them first and even make some reference to them, however brief, in his synopsis. Otherwise he might forget something important and either make more work for himself or produce an inferior book. So I would suggest we discuss these extra elements before we talk about the actual writing of the novel itself.

ILLUSTRATION 6: Story-line development

The theme has now spawned a plot; the cast is assembled; the setting chosen.

A more detailed synopsis at this stage can break the story into chapters, or easily handled sections, to ensure an even flow of narrative and inclusion of vital points.

Chapter

1 Wife waiting Dr's verdict
Family background — scene set
James' state of mind?

2 Tension building as family
members reveal attitudes to
his illness. Undertones of
things not as they seem.
Mother/daughter-in-law relations.

3 James & Dr return. James in a
mood. (HAS) to work!! *Drives himself*

4 Dr's verdict. No guarantee on
op's outcome. Wife's choice.
Husband incapable of decision.

~~6~~ Wife has to tell family.
Eruptions of self-interest.
Divisions.

5 ~~6~~ Reasoning behind choice. *Pique!!*

7 James & Mary. Rational spell.
Sudden outburst of ferocious
anger — means Mary quarrels
with his mother — again!

8 Gwen suspects her sister of
having affair with her husband.
Provokes outburst in James by
playing his special waltz.

9 James' sister tries to force
Jealous of Mary; married state Dr to insist on op. Suspects
his ulterior motives (interest
in wife?)Mary clutches at
straws in unearthing James'
guilt to save him.

10 Mary persuades Dr to postpone
any decision for a week.

11 What is the truth about Stella's
life James' dead brother?

Chapter

12 Interlude — more smouldering
quarrels. Frank loves Stella?

13 Party. Frank persuades Mary & *Party at home, but hosted by Gwen*
James to be there. Gwen plays
his music on purpose — to air
her suspicions.

14 Time running out for Mary's
decision. James' sister wants
a second opinion on op to force
Dr to agree to it.

15 James realises his mind has
dark fears. As he glimpses
his own secret he tries to
commit suicide.

16 Stella and Frank save him.

17 They take him home and call Dr
(~~Gwen~~) tells Frank that Stella *Pique!!*
and James had an affair while
David away in war. Frank thinks
this could be James' guilt.

18 He tells Mary who decides to
confront James with it. Frank
wants Dr there — but can't find
him — drives off.

19 He and Dr can't get back
and are delayed.

20 Mary decides not to wait for Dr
She confronts James who makes a
homicidal attack on her. *And Stella*

~~21~~ 22 Aftermath — James set to
recover. Has he faced his
guilt? Can Dr declare any
interest in Mary? *No*

~~22~~ 21 *Stella disfigured. Frank
has proved himself capable,
despite his war wound. Declares
himself to her. She is at
peace as well.*

7   Suspense and Conflict

In reading some of your reviews, I notice your ability to create suspense is frequently mentioned. What are your views on it and how do you go about achieving it?

Suspense is a critically important factor in any fictional work. It can be called dramatic content and also readability, because that is the effect it has. To make a reader want to keep on turning over the pages when he is uncomfortably aware he has an appointment or has to rise early in the morning.

In a novel it is achieved in two ways: through the thematic structure of the book, which of course includes the inter-reaction of the characters, and through the events within the story, which include the dialogue.

This doesn't mean a book must have a thrill on every page. As I said earlier, the aim in the story-line is to have a steady rise in tension with minor crises on the way. In other words an ascending graph with crises here and there until the final climax is reached. The crises should fascinate but never be overdone or the reader will be sated by too much excitement. The climax should always overshadow what has happened before and the denouement should be short, or an anticlimax will be produced.

Suspense, or tension, isn't the same as mystery, but both aspects have a function in the novel. Many of your own novels employ both simultaneously, but is suspense always an essential and mystery only an optional accessory in a general novel?

Suspense, as against mystery, should exist in every novel, whether it be a thriller or a straight novel. What will differ will be the way it is handled. In a thriller it will generally take more graphic forms while in the straight novel it will be handled more subtly, by hints and nuances of speech and behaviour although, of course, these ploys can also be used in thrillers. So much depends on the quality of a novel. But suspense, or a rising graph of tension if you wish, should be present in every dramatic work.

Mystery, on the other hand, need not exist, although if introduced it can add an extra dimension to the suspense already present. In some works, however, as in Agatha Christie's novels, mystery is used as the main plotting element and because of the reader's need to find out 'who dun it' a kind of suspense is created.

Can you provide examples from your own work?

Most of the 633 SQUADRON novels fit the first category. Because of their structure, the details of the main operation were known relatively early to the reader, if not to the aircrews, and so the mystery of the main target was eliminated. This meant it was even more important that suspense and tension were on a high level to compensate. This I tried to achieve by the crews having special training which allowed reader identification. He, the reader, was allowed to share in the crews' thoughts, hardships, dangers and fears and, as their tension became screwed up almost to breaking point, my hope was that the reader would share some of that tension.

But surely you used mystery in the sixth of the series, OPERATION TITAN?

Yes. When writing a series of books of this nature, one has to change the formula occasionally, so in OPERATION TITAN I deliberately made the target a mystery, my reason being that if the Germans learned of it they would guess where the invasion would take place. Thus not even Group Headquarters could know of its nature. To heighten the mystery I devised certain obstacles that the crews were ordered to fly through during their training. As some of these obstacles were grotesque as well as dangerous, they served to provide humour (through the crews' comments) as well as mystery and suspense that (hopefully) lasted almost to the climax of the story.

You've mentioned the importance of conflict in relation to structuring the plot. Will you amplify its role and give more examples of its use?

It can be produced through a conflict of situations or a conflict of characters. In the former case a man or woman might be torn between two or more decisions which might affect their entire lives. In the latter, the more common case, it can be produced by the confrontation of characters different in their beliefs, personalities, and backgrounds.

This use of conflicting personalities was a ploy I used in the second of the 633 SQUADRON novels, OPERATION RHINE MAIDEN. It was a very difficult novel to write because in the original novel almost all the major characters had been killed. This made a sequel a real problem and it was not until I remembered that a number of the original crews had been wounded and hospitalised, that I was able to develop a synopsis.

The plot now went this way. The 'old sweats', by this time fully recovered, formed the core of the rebuilt squadron while 'freshers' were brought in to bring up its establishment. With the contempt veterans always have for beginners, I now had ample scope for bitter quarrels, particularly as one of my old sweats was a Northerner with strong Socialist tendencies, while the Squadron Commander, brought in over his head, came from the privileged classes.

It was now possible to build these internecine quarrels into the main story-line, which I believe made the novel more powerful. It was also very satisfying to show how high stress could bridge the previously unbridgeable social gaps that had lain between my two main protagonists.

Are there other ways a plot can produce mystery and/or suspense?

Yes. One can create characters whose personalities produce these elements. They can be people of great charm, charismatic figures in fact, and yet the writer can hint in subtle ways that they have a darker, more sinister side to their natures.

That would apply to quite a number of your characters, men like the charismatic Seymour in your award-winning novel, A KILLING FOR THE HAWKS, set during the First World War?

It certainly was my intention to use him this way. I made him handsome, aristocratic, a natural leader of men, and an ace pilot. His men worship him and so, at first, does a young Canadian volunteer, Norman McConnell, who in the beginning accepts Seymour's ruthless behaviour towards the enemy as a natural adjunct of war. Then McConnell falls in love with Seymour's wife and is told about the real Seymour who enjoys giving her physical pain and who treasures the souvenirs he takes from men he has killed. When Seymour finds out the two are having an affair, the nightmare begins for McConnell.

However, Seymour's revenge is not the simple one the reader might expect. In this kind of story - in any kind of story - characters must be true to themselves. Seymour is an intelligent, imaginative sadist, and too subtle to strike at McConnell personally. Instead, he uses a psychological punishment that is far more painful and devastating.

In other words suspense and tension throughout the story are all produced from Seymour's character.

Would that method apply just as well if one used a character in a reverse way? That is showing eventually that rude or unprepossessing characters aren't as bad as they are first painted?

Yes. A man or woman can be introduced showing a hard or even criminal side to the reader and yet can be seen later to have a soft centre or even to be playing a double role. Although at first glance this would seem to weaken a story - it being generally assumed in literary work that evil is more powerful than good - this does not apply if the plot has an active base. This, of course, was the method I used in THE WAR GOD. At first my German leader, Kessler, appears to be a man without scruples. However, tiny incidents hint he is more complex than he pretends to be. So when the truth does come out, it is a climax in itself, quite apart from the climax of the main story-line.

These are just a few examples of how construction of a novel and the selection of characters can introduce mystery and suspense throughout the entire work. Of course there are other ways they can be achieved. As I have said, the detective story does it mostly by the mystery of 'who dun it?' The thriller by the chase and the confrontation. The romance by whether or not the would-be lovers ever make it. And so on.

The need for a suspenseful plot applies equally to so-called straight novels but one doesn't always find it. For a long time I've believed English literature is splitting apart. On the one hand there are the genre novels, often with plenty of action and suspense but more often than not with cardboard characters. On the other hand there are the straight novels whose characters might be convincing enough but whose pages are boring to read because necessary plotting elements are missing. One wonders why both sides don't come together and produce books that have credible characters within a framework that stimulates and excites. Excitement, after all, doesn't need to come from physical action. It can be equally effective when it excites the mind. To achieve this, however, the writer must not despise the art of story-telling.

So far we've only been talking about the creation of suspense by the story-line or the chosen characters. What about the suspense 'within' the story-line to highlight the peaks and troughs demanded by the plot? What are the tricks used to produce this effect?

A writer must use his imagination here. We all know how useful the weather can be - the hush before the storm, the distant lightning, the low growl of thunder as a warning. But topography can also be used. A plant or a scene can be described so cleverly that it suggests approaching menace. Animals or insects can be used in the same way, such as a snake coiled as if about to strike or a stick insect about to catch its prey.

Such tricks are useful in that they create atmosphere and a setting without slowing down the pace of the story itself. For it must be remembered that if one is writing thrillers or their like, pace is everything. Halting the action to describe a scene or pausing while a person thinks something out are elements that should only be introduced if they are part of the story-line itself and help to keep it moving. That, of course, is one reason why one seldom gets good characterisation in this kind of novel. Only experts can paint credible characters in quick brushstrokes while those characters are hurling themselves around or doing deeds of astonishing valour.

Perhaps it is fortunate that readers of this kind of fiction don't seem too critical of their heroes.

How, then, would you sum up this section on suspense?

Suspense, or the art of drama if you like, is an absolute essential of story-telling and is the skill a fiction writer must develop. He can, unfortunately, get away with cardboard characters but he can't get away with a story that lacks suspense-making elements. Without them and good characters, there is nothing left to hold the reader.

My advice is to read as much well-written fiction as one can. The elements will be easy to recognise in the action-packed thrillers, the Gothics, the horror stories, and even in the light romances. They will be less easy to spot in the good literary novels, but make no mistake, they will still be there although now their form will take the shape of nuances in conversation, glances, subtle hints, and so on.

Dramatic suspense is the element that prevents the reader from turning off his bedside lamp. Unless a writer possesses a natural gift for drama, it must be learned before he can hope to be a novelist, and it will be a great help to him to study how published writers handle it. But do remember it is not only the classics that have suspense. The hyped best-sellers, with their often banal themes, would have no way of surviving without it, even if it does sometimes appear in its crudest form. But for a beginner learning his trade, this might be no bad thing.

ILLUSTRATION 7: Putting in the conflict

The plot calls for major and mini crises. The injection of suspense is vital to heighten the tension. But the novel should not maintain this high level throughout, so the screw must be turned only at certain moments.

Levels of suspense:

1 The composer's unstable state of mind. His unpredictable and violent moods cast a shadow over all their lives. *Recurrent throughout. Heralded by music esp 8.* — *Big scene Chapter 3*

2 The mother's very strong maternal love – at the expense of all other family members. Leads to conflict with daughter-in-law when both believe they want what's best for James. *Sub conflict Mother/wife, lesser tension than husband/wife*

3 If James and Mary live in the family home (the mother's) the wife will feel a greater stress in wanting to get him away from the suffocating atmosphere. *Feeling trapped only surfaces occasionally*

3 The operation's uncertain outcome puts great stress on all concerned – especially the wife.

4 The past guilt: was there an affair between James and Stella whilst her husband (his brother) was in the RAF? If so, did James know it was her? *Not at the time. (Never met the war-time bride)* Does James feel guilty because David was killed shortly afterwards? *Think's it's punishment for a night's sin!!*

5 The Doctor is an old family friend, with a hidden love for Mary – but if James' sister suspects this, she will misconstrue their closeness. This she will use in order to prevent Mary letting her brother go mad, rather than saving him, to go to her 'lover'. *Must always be above board and innocent.*

6 Stella's half sister and brother-in-law (Mervyn). She is dazzling (though flippant) and Mervyn pursues her – and his wife is incensed. Frank (James's brother) would like to pursue her. Ethel (the sister) jealous of Stella's sexual attractiveness, and Mary's financially secure life, is eager to find a reason to put one over on Stella and safeguard James from Mary. *Mini-crises to alleviate main tension, but excite* Ø

7 Time will be a very important element – that makes the decision and the race for a solution much more sinister and heart-rending.

Ø *Frank's 'redemption' via saving the women's lives*

8   Viewpoint

Viewpoint is often likened to the camera through which the action is seen. Would you agree with that as a definition?

Yes, I think it is a good one. As a novel develops, the action within its covers is seen through the 'camera' or eyes of one or another of its characters. In theory this can include as many characters as the novel contains but in general these differing views are limited to the main characters.

It does not cease with vision, of course. While a character is seeing an incident, he is also thinking about it, so thought and vision go hand in hand. As the reader is always sharing the same 'camera' as these characters, he is also sharing their reactions too. That is the aspect of writing called viewpoint.

Is the choice of viewpoint a conscious one on your part, or does it naturally evolve as the plot takes shape, with one or more predominant characters claiming attention?

It's a conscious one but the way it is handled isn't always clear-cut in the beginning. It depends firstly whether I'm going to write the novel in the 1st or 3rd person. If it is in the 1st person, there is no problem. The viewpoint must stay with the story-teller because, like the rest of us, he can only know his own thoughts and guess at everyone else's. So the viewpoint will always be his alone.

If I've decided on the 3rd person, however, when I have the freedom to know and express the thoughts of everyone in my story if I wish, then we have to narrow our definitions down to the scenes and conversations that occur within the structure of the novel. We might have two people talking in a room and need to know the thoughts of each. Unless a writer is very skilful, it becomes too clumsy to give each other's responses to every line of dialogue, so the answer is to keep the viewpoint with one of the characters for a certain length of time and then switch the viewpoint to the other. As it's not always possible to set all these situations down in a synopsis, I tend to make my decisions on viewpoint when I'm actually writing the story.

That brings up two questions for beginners, who always find the switching of viewpoint difficult. Must viewpoint only involve main characters? And how long should each hold the stage?

Viewpoint does usually stay with the main characters but situations do sometimes arise when the reader needs to know the thoughts of minor characters too. If he does, the viewpoint switch has to be made.

As for length, many writers allow a character to hold viewpoint for a chapter before making the switch. It is a neat formula but if a writer uses long chapters, a character might hold the stage too long for the good of the story. For myself, I often make the switch within a chapter if I think it necessary. The important thing to remember is to make it quite clear to the reader who is now 'holding the camera'.

But when a writer can't leave the viewpoint solely with one character, is it practical or easy to switch backwards and forwards?

When I wrote my novel called THE OBSESSION, it dealt with the bitter-sweet love affair between a young woman newspaper reporter and an older man who won a decoration against the Nazis in the last war. Because the man, a war hero, has recently become a member of a new Fascist party, the girl's newspaper assigns her to find out the reason for his astonishing switch.

The girl, hating Fascism in all its guises, is convinced she detests everything the man stands for. But in trying to find out why he has made this volte-face, she discovers to her horror that she is falling in love with him. Consequently, as she pretends friendship to gain his confidence, she discovers that almost every word she speaks becomes a lie as her mind finds fault with the things he says back to her. Yet while this is happening her body wants him.

He, equally in love with her, has to indulge in the same sophistry, although for different reasons. The outcome is that much of their dialogue is deceit, with them saying one thing and thinking another. This forced me to change my viewpoint at almost every sentence because it would have been far too clumsy to have gone back later to explain the real thoughts behind every statement.

This is an example of how difficult it is to set down hard and fast rules for writers. At the same time this does not mean that rules cannot be useful as guidelines.

To recap on viewpoint, allow one character to retain the viewpoint for a section or a chapter of the novel in normal circumstances but don't be afraid to make the switch more frequently if the situation demands it.

1ST PERSON OR 3RD PERSON

In the context of viewpoint, what are your feelings about the choice of 1st or 3rd person when plotting a novel? Do you have a preference for one voice rather than the other?

The choice depends so much on the idea for each book. Some ideas are too complicated to be told in the 1st person, they demand to know the thoughts of its different characters before the plot can be worked out. In such cases the 3rd person must be used when structuring the story. The problem arises in the in-between cases when it's feasible to handle the plot in one way or the other. Then the writer has to pause and give the matter careful thought.

You have successfully used the 1st person in your novel LYDIA TRENDENNIS and also in two of your thrillers, THE DEVIL BEHIND ME and THE STORM KNIGHT. Is this because you felt reader association would heighten the excitement?

Yes. When it's possible to use it, I like the 1st person. It has one great advantage. Because it is the writer making all the statements, he can introduce thoughts and ideas into the narrative without holding up the story-line, as tends to happen in 3rd person novels. It is also excellent for reader identification because the reader in a sense becomes the narrator, and if the novel is done well he suffers all the narrator's joys and pains to the same degree. In addition, as we have just said, it obviates all the viewpoint problems.

But it has many drawbacks. Remember first of all, that with only one viewpoint available, every scene or conversation in the story must be witnessed or heard by the narrator, unless he is told about it by other characters. This oblique approach is useful but it can't be used very often because it tends to be cumbersome and to intrude on the action. In the main the narrator has to be wherever a writer's story-line takes him. In one way it is a natural thing because that is what happens in real life. But in a novel it presents many problems.

The narrator can't, for example, know what others are thinking unless they tell him, and even then he can't be certain they are telling him the truth. Equally, he can't know what they are doing if they are off stage. It strips away writer omniscience completely and so makes plotting more difficult. Yet on the whole I favour it if the plot is suitable.

This is the real issue. Some plots, the more complicated ones, simply could not be developed in the 1st person. They need the different viewpoints of the protagonists to build up the drama. It is the simpler kind of story - the woman telling the reader about her husband's infidelity, the man talking about his war experiences - when the 1st person comes into its own.

We have to return to the premise then that 1st person is very effective, but hard for a novice to handle?

Effective, yes, but it is difficult for the beginner. Its pitfalls are not always obvious when the synopsis is drawn up and only become apparent when the writing has begun, which can then be very costly in time and effort. The entire story-line might have to be changed and new characters added when the writer discovers his hero or heroine isn't able to play a full part in the action.

The 3rd person, on the other hand, can be used in any plot. In the more complex story it allows the writer to be wherever his characters are, to hear all the conversations that he wants his readers to hear, and, most importantly of all, to know their thoughts. The advantage here is that while he allows Character A to say something politely to Character B, he can let his reader know that Character A's private thoughts are anything but polite. Subtleties of this nature are much more difficult to convey in the 1st person.

Perhaps a useful simile is a television or film script. Because they are working in a visual medium, playwrights suffer all the time from the problems of the 1st person. They cannot convey what their characters are thinking and so have to resort to all kinds of trickery and subtle dialogue. A novelist using the 3rd person has an immense advantage over playwrights when handling a complex theme, and it seems foolhardy to throw it away unless he is a master dramatist. And even then the sacrifice is often pointless.

To sum up, then, I would advise the new writer to use the 3rd person in his earlier books, even if his story is a simple one (when 'he' or 'she' simply replaces 'I'), but to keep in mind the power of the 1st person when his experience grows and his skills develop.

ILLUSTRATION 8: Who's telling the story?

The focal point for the story-telling needs choosing with care: many stories can be told from differing angles - some can't!

Main characters

James	Mary	Mother	Stella	Doctor
Going mad and not able to be rational or lucid.	Strong and very anxious to do the best for her husband.	Matriarchal Wants her son at all costs – even if it ruins his ability to create.	Involved but in the main with James	Objective or is he? His love for Mary will make him very suspect.
Could he hold a viewpoint?	She can be the mirror of everyone's fears and traumas.		Can she see enough of the picture?	
		Her view is very narrow and self-orientated.		
	She can become the whipping boy for the family.			

Too difficult and a distorted view of life

The trauma revolves round her

Neither can be totally objective. Neither directly involved in the conflict

Viewpoint changes?

Minor characters in sub-stories?

Frank, Stella and Gwen will have to contribute their stories of the past – via small changes of viewpoint. Sub-plots will need viewpoint changes.

1st or 3rd? — allows differing viewpoints

First, much too restrictive. Much will depend on James's state of mind being seen and discussed by all the other characters and especially the immediate family.

9   Time

I've heard you say that time causes novelists more headaches than almost anything else. Why is this?

Looking back, I think it's caused me more problems than finding ideas, developing plots, and creating characters put together. Lately I've realised that is because many of my novels could be called *faction* - that means stories written around factual happenings when time is a fixed ingredient - but even in traditional novels when one is free to juggle about with all the elements, it can still cause headaches.

Is the problem, then, more one of fitting the novel into the time, or the time into the novel?

I believe it's the former. The first thing a writer should decide is the time-scale of his novel, whether it is going to take place in a month, a year, ten years or whatever. Then, into that overall limit, he fits his incidents, after deciding their appropriate lengths.

This sounds relatively simple until he starts facing the natural time-scales of life, such as the term of a woman's pregnancy. The story-line he has decided on might not allow a nine month interlude but if only for the poor girl's comfort, he can't stretch it to eighteen months or reduce it to three. I had this problem in my novel LAWS BE THEIR ENEMY and it took me over a month to solve. Something else in the plot had to be changed and that in turn led to another change and so on. So even this method sometimes presents problems.

Can you recommend ways to deal with these problems? A family tree, for instance, or a chronological list?

If one is writing a saga stretching over decades, then a family tree is a great help. One should also ensure no planned incident runs longer than its time-scale allows. It is also a help to list the major happenings that occurred during the period covered by the novel. These sometimes provide ideas that can be incorporated into the story-line. They can be obtained from one of those books that lists in chronological order the major events of the decades or century.

But with the number of permutations that the time problem causes, it's impossible to give specific advice without seeing a writer's synopsis. Nevertheless, there are a number of preparatory steps he should always take. He should take great care over the structure of his synopsis, checking the age of his characters and the years they are on his stage. In this context he must remember the frequency of wars and how they could tear couples apart when his story-line might require them to be together. He should check that the professions or occupations of his main characters would not have been affected by such things as strikes or disasters which occurred during the time span of his novel. And so on.

To be honest, much of this is commonsense but it is surprising the tangle we all get into over time. A writer will obviate the worst problems if he gives careful thought to time when structuring his synopsis, yet I'll lay odds he will still meet some when he is actually writing the novel. The reason, of course, is that we are trying to make shape and sense out of life whereas life itself - at least to us - seems to possess neither.

Is there another way round the tedious repetition when paragraphs start such as 'six months passed and then . . '?

This does get repetitious and is also clumsy. Instead, I tend to use the white line or double space. This acts like the cut in a film script and indicates either a change of time or a change of locale. It is still necessary to explain what the change is at some later date but it does do away with clumsy explanations when the cut is being made and so allows the reader to go straight into the next scene.

FLASHBACKS

One very important aspect of time in novels is the handling of flashbacks. How do you approach this difficult area?

Flashbacks are, of course, recollections of past events, often brought into a novel to clarify or progress the story-line or explain a character's behaviour.

It can't be denied that it is better to do without them altogether if one can help it. The time to decide this is when the synopsis is being planned and constructed. But avoidance is not always easy and in some involved synopses it is quite impossible.

In such a case, what methods do you use to get round the problem?

One way is for the writer to slip in a piece of information in the midst of a narrative passage. If done well and briefly, the reader will barely notice he has been fed past information but it will nevertheless be recorded in his mind. It is commonly used but it has the drawback most flashbacks suffer from of holding up the story unless it is very brief and in turn this limits the amount of information it can convey.

If there is no way of avoiding a lengthy flashback using this method, then a tip here is to use the pluperfect tense (the 'had had') no more than a couple of times and then revert to the ordinary past tense. If the flashback is kept to a minimum number of paragraphs, the reader should have no trouble in realising it all relates to the same scene.

Then there is the reflective method - the character, seeing some nostalgic object or smelling an evocative scent, being taken down memory lane back to some relevant incident in his life. It can be effective if used well but again it does tend to check the movement of the story. This can be overcome in most straight novels but it is a real handicap if one is writing a thriller, when reflections should be cut down to the bone.

Would you favour the old standby, the dream scene, as a viable flashback alternative?

It can be useful, particularly if it is a nightmare reminding a man of previous danger. This can work well in a thriller because it can be made exciting in its own right. But clearly it can't be used more than once (unless it is the same dream which has a bearing on the story-line). A neurotic hero having endless nightmares isn't hardly likely to inspire a reader with confidence!

Conversation about the past is often used. Is this acceptable?

When written skilfully, it is one of the best ways of handling a flashback and it avoids the use of the pluperfect tense which all writers find difficult.

There is one method you haven't mentioned and that is the very different way you handled time in THE OBSESSION.

It's interesting that you have noticed this because not one critic made mention of it. In the novel it was vital that the personality of the main character, Tom Reid, should be shown to the reader in every guise possible. To do this I decided to describe his life in four periods, his life as a child, his wartime experiences, his life in the Sixties and his life today. The book itself - the upper layer as it were - I wrote in the present and in the normal 3rd person. However, when I wanted to do a flashback, instead of using any of the conventional methods, I simply started a new chapter about him in that period and wrote it in exactly the same way as the present one. The same tense, the same everything.

The only time I used the memory method was about his childhood. His war and his life in the Sixties were both presented as stories in themselves. They were not written concurrently. One chapter takes the reader so far along that period, the next brings him back to the present. Then something happens in the present that needs an earlier explanation and so the next chapter of the earlier series returns. In effect the chapters on the war and the Sixties could be plucked out and joined together, when they would make almost complete stories in themselves.

In the way they are used, they hopefully give more power to the story-line that is the forefront of the novel. Another advantage of this method, of course, is that the three stories could be written so that they all join together near the end of the book and produce a more powerful climax.

Of course few books need or would be improved by this kind of structure and I mention it only because it is a fifth alternative when the other methods do not work. I confess I have not seen it used before although one feels it must have been because what is new in the world? I admit I did hold my breath when the reviews came in but when no one mentioned the method, much less criticised it, I feel it must have worked.

FORESHADOWING

The opposite to flashback is the foreshadowing of events still to come. Does this entail a risk of giving away the plot?

Foreshadowing is a device by which seeds of eventual happenings, that are to prove important later, are planted in the story. The reader is fed them almost subliminally, and they give him a sense of discovery and a 'why-didn't-I-think-of-that' feeling when the outcome of the story is revealed.

Detective stories, of course, could not exist without such clues being dropped, and they give the plot away only if the writer lacks the skill to make them seem innocuous. But foreshadowing is used in many types of novels because of its satisfying effect on the reader.

Would you agree that time can be a legitimate plot element in its own right, as a device to create suspense?

Most definitely. One comes across this formula many times in the thriller type of novel where the hero (or heroes) has only so long to find a killer before the killer's victim appears in a public place where he will become a sitting target. Or a suspense novel in which the hero must find a bomb before it has time to explode and destroy a ship or an aircraft.

Another example could be a doctor working against time to prevent a virulent disease becoming a widespread epidemic. Or a surgeon working against time to save a patient. In all such cases and many more, time becomes the major element in creating tension and suspense.

Can you give an example from one of your own novels?

I don't have to go farther than OF MASKS AND MINDS. The knowledge that her husband's mental condition could collapse into total madness at any time added enormously to the wife's stress in trying to find the guilt that caused it.

As a final point on the subject of time, how important is it to establish when the action of the novel is taking place? Should it be explicitly shown or should the reader just 'work it out' for himself.

So much depends on the novel that is being written. Occasionally a writer does not want the reader to associate his novel with any particular time, feeling the subject he is handling is timeless. In such a case he will leave out all the factors that could peg his novel to a time and leave his readers to choose their own.

But in the majority of novels, even if no dates are given, the reader is usually able to identify the time by the characters' actions and speech and the social conditions in which they operate. In these cases it is up to the writer whether he wants to define the date precisely or not. In most cases it makes little or no difference.

ILLUSTRATION 9: Setting the clock

The time-scale of the novel is the restrictive framework in which the events happen.

It can be a legitimate plot element, adding to the suspense - but the chronology must be right.

Question

Possibilities

What time is it set? — Contemporary - 1950ish — *otherwise he'd be locked away as mad*

Should it look at all James' life? — Not necessary

His career as composer? — Revealed by his family

Gradually reveal his madness? — *That's apparent*

⊗ Should wartime adultery be included — Yes — *crux of his guilt*

If so: how? *By Gwen, in a fit of pique. But not as flashbacks — if reader doesn't see James doing it, the extent of his guilt & ... is better hidden (for him)*

If wife resists committal, how long should the story continue? — Fairly tight to make it urgent

Where to start:
Some time prior to Dr's verdict?
✳ Immediately prior? — *Build up of tension — wondering what? Set scene*
Verdict being delivered? — Could be dramatic spot

Overall time scale? — Very short, adds to the growing claustrophobia Heightens tension — *One week - broken into uneven lengths*

Length of action? — ~~A month~~
A week
24 hours? *Too short to contain all the action*

⊗ Flashbacks — to war? *No* — Episodic format, cut in to past scenes.

Ages: Mother *born 1885 (65)*

Mary = James   Frank   Ethel=Dick   David = Stella
b1920 b1915   b1919   b1910   b1922   b1920
(30)   (35)   (31)   (40)   died '44 (30)
                             b1900
                             (50)

10   Dialogue

Dialogue seems to be another area that presents the novice with all kinds of difficulties when it comes to actually writing it on the page. Has that been your experience?

It does seem a common problem. Perhaps because so many novice writers don't realise that literary dialogue is quite different to spoken dialogue, that is we do not write the way we speak. One has only to stop and listen to anyone talking to understand why. We pause, mutter, use the wrong words, repeat ourselves - a novel full of such mumbo jumbo would be unbelievably boring. What we writers have to do is give the *impression* of natural conversation while at the same time getting our statements over in as efficient a way as possible.

This is why literary dialogue can seldom be used in plays or in films adapted from a book. Read in print, it seems perfectly natural if the author knows his job. Read aloud, its artificiality immediately becomes apparent.

For this reason some authors find it almost impossible to become playwrights and vice versa. The technique is quite different and with some people very difficult to learn. I have read books in which the narrative is excellent and the dialogue awkward and stilted. Then one gets the reverse, good dialogue and poor descriptions. The latter writer ought perhaps to have aimed at television or the theatre because, of course, in scripts for those media one only needs dialogue. There is no doubt that most writers in their early days are better at one or the other.

The writer should know where his strengths and weaknesses lie and if he finds dialogue easy and narrative difficult, he might consider these alternatives to novel writing. If he is determined to write novels, however, then he must master both techniques.

This difficulty of handling speech means people like myself have to spend a great deal of time helping students to get it right. What would you recommend?

Reading books by good novelists is essential here but the following suggestions might be of help.

One should try as much as possible to have the dialogues of one's characters match their education and intelligence. This is not only necessary to establish their backgrounds but it also serves to reveal their characters without lengthy descriptions which, for reasons mentioned elsewhere, are not favoured. This use is one of the great virtues of dialogue and can define characters as acutely as their actions can.

Let me give an example. A Scotsman wakes up one morning to find his wife lying dead in bed alongside him. Frowning, he shouts downstairs to his housekeeper. "Only one boiled egg this morning, Martha!" An absurd example, of course, but I think it makes the point.

Wherever possible, keep statements short and crisp. Unless one is deliberately trying to make a character long-winded, terse dialogue is always preferable if the information being imparted allows it.

If it does not, then the statement should appear in one paragraph if possible, although the dialogue can be broken, like this:

> *This time he shrugged. "I've nothing to stop me now. My son's living in Australia and my daughter's up in Scotland." Suddenly his eyes looked bleak. "I wouldn't say either has a call to keep me down in Dorset, would you?"*

SETTING OUT DIALOGUE

Although examples are everywhere, students seem to find the setting out of dialogue and its punctuation very difficult. What is your advice?

Almost certainly the same as yours. Look into almost any published book or magazine to find examples galore. However, I do agree punctuation does cause great problems. In the example I've just given the small break for narrative runs straight on with the dialogue. On the other hand, if the speech has to be long, then the quotation mark at the end of each paragraph should be omitted, although it should be used at the beginning of the next paragraph, which should be indented. In this way:

> *"It happened in 1944," Mary said, "after Stella and David had been married for nearly a year. Stella was staying with Gwen, in a flat in London. At that time she had met none of your family. She hadn't seen David for months and was bored and lonely.*
>
> *"She wanted to join up but the Food Ministry wouldn't release her. A few weeks before D-Day, Gwen went away for a fortnight's holiday with Mervyn, leaving Stella alone in the flat. During that time Stella heard from one of David's friends that James was on leave.*
>
> *"I remember that leave well," Mary went on quietly. "James had only been given two days leave, and I was in Northern Ireland at the time. There was no chance of our meeting and so he told me*

by letter that he would spend the leave in London with some friends.''

(Of Masks and Minds)

It is the omission of the quote at the end of each paragraph that tells a reader the character's speech has not yet ended. The reason more than one paragraph is used, of course, is to prevent the entire speech looking too long and heavy on the page.

Equally, when another character speaks, the writer should indent as he would for any new paragraph. As I've said, almost any novel illustrates how dialogue is set out, which makes it difficult to understand why this aspect of writing should cause so many problems.

SHOULD ONE USE DIALECT?

So-termed 'regional' novels, in which culture and dialect set their characters in a precise location, are once again popular. Would you advocate employing dialect for their characters or is there an easy way to avoid this?

I personally detest dialect novels. To begin with I find them extremely difficult to read. Also, to write them, you need an actor's ear for accents and I don't have one. Nor, to be honest, do I think much dialect is necessary.

My solution is to announce early on in the story that so-and-so is a Yorkshireman and so-and-so is a Scot and leave the reader to do the rest with his inner ear. Of course you jog him along with the occasional "By Gum," or "Och Aye," but it really isn't necessary or sensible to change the spelling of almost every word. The trick is to put more emphasis on phrasing than on dialect. By that I mean the way a Scot or an American will put the words of his sentences together in a different sequence to those of a Yorkshireman. It might only be the re-arrangement of a word here and there but that is sufficient to remind the reader which man is which. In addition the general speech and behaviour of the characters ought to give a constant clue to their nationalities.

HANDLING THE FOREIGNER

As with dialect, many beginners feel it necessary to use foreign, and often unintelligible, words when other nationals are speaking, as an attempt at realism. I would avoid it, would you?

It should be handled in the same way as dialect, by using the grammatical order in the appropriate language. Spanish, for example, has no apostrophe, so the possessive has to be stated in full, e.g. it is the house of Senor Smith. Likewise, German usually places the verb at the end of the sentence, e.g. every traveller money needs. Here words are all English and readily understandable, but the character is obviously foreign.

Equally, a French or Italian writer would employ the same method when writing about an Englishman or an American.

KEEPING IT TAUT

As we agree, everyday conversation is peppered with irrelevances, with 'ums' and 'ers'. These have to be eliminated on the page, haven't they?

Dialogue must be kept to the point. It is frighteningly easy to waffle on and fill pages with dialogue and hardly move the story along one inch. Even if one is deliberately making a character's conversation *appear* trite, it should still be handled in a way that aids the story's progression. This, of course, applies to narrative too. In an ideal novel, every printed word should serve this purpose.

WHEN TO USE DIALOGUE

A line of dialogue can say a great deal in a few words. Is that a reasonable way of effectively tightening and shortening a book?

Yes, dialogue can dramatically shorten a book if used correctly. Sometimes one runs into objects or situations so complicated to describe they might take a full page or more of narrative. See how much quicker they can be drawn by a character talking about them. Moreover, the result is so much easier to read.

HOW MUCH DIALOGUE IS PERMISSIBLE?

How much dialogue would a good balanced novel contain, then? Is too little better than too much?

I feel it is quite the reverse, that one can't have too much dialogue if it is crisp and informative because it is so much easier to read than great chunks of narrative. It's difficult to give a suitable proportion as so much depends on the story-line of a book. However, I suppose an average dialogue content would be around thirty per cent, although I wouldn't put fifty per cent too high if it were of good quality.

Indeed, dialogue can be very useful in shortening a work. I once had an idea for a novel that I realised from the beginning would be extremely long if I wrote it with the average percentage of narrative and dialogue. Not wanting this length, I determined from the outset I would include much more dialogue than usual. As a result the length was cut by over a third. I believe the book, A MEETING OF STARS, turned out a better, more readable novel.

THE BELOVED ADVERB!

Overwriting is a persistently common fault in work that I assess.

Too many unnecessary words. Where should the novice wield the blue pencil?

We've all read novels full of these: *"Stop," John said hurriedly. "I don't like it," the child cried plaintively. "I think it's marvellous, absolutely marvellous," Janet said admiringly,* and so on. In nearly all such cases one finds these adverbs are unnecessary because of the narrative or conversation that precedes them. Moreover they give an amateurish effect to the writing. The only time one needs adverbs are in explanations such as: *"Be careful, he could be listening," Joan said quietly.* Otherwise he said or she said is sufficient and even this verb is often only necessary to give a balance to dialogue. In most cases the alternating paragraphs by themselves tell a reader who is speaking, even if the dialogue itself doesn't. Again, one should read good novelists but in this case not the old ones, no matter how famous their names. They loved their verbs and adverbs far too much.

Can you show by example how cutting the adverbs and extraneous words can tighten and improve the quality of dialogue?

I'll try. This is a conversation of a man trying to find out from a nursing sister how his hospitalised father is progressing.

First draft:

At that point the ward sister broke in impatiently. "Mr Maxwell is a very busy surgeon. We are here to answer any questions from relatives. What exactly do you want to know?"

"I've just told you," Reid said. "I'm trying to find out what condition my father is in for the operation."

"He's as good as can be expected, Mr Reid," the ward sister said stiffly. "Otherwise Mr Maxwell wouldn't be operating."

"Yes, but how good is that?" Reid asked. "A couple of weeks ago I was told his chances of getting through the operation were only fifty fifty. I was hoping you might have been able to build him up a little since he's been with you."

There were red spots in the ward sister's cheeks now. "We've done everything possible, Mr Reid."

"Yes, I'm sure you have," Reid said appeasingly. "But a few days ago he was given some tests to establish the condition of his arteries and I was wondering if the results were more encouraging."

The same conversation as redrafted:

At that point the ward sister broke in. "Mr Maxwell is a very busy surgeon. We are here to answer any questions from relatives. What exactly do you want to know?"

"I've just told you. I'm trying to find out what condition my father is in for the operation."

"He's as good as can be expected, Mr Reid. Otherwise Mr Maxwell wouldn't be operating."

"Yes, but how good is that? A couple of weeks ago I was told his chances of getting through the operation were only fifty fifty. I was hoping you might have been able to build him up a little since he's been with you."

"We've done everything possible, Mr Reid."

"Yes, I'm sure you have. But a few days ago he was given some tests to establish the condition of his arteries and I was wondering if the results were more encouraging."

(The Obsession)

Notice that it is not only adjectives and adverbs that can be unnecessary and clutter up dialogue but also verbs and statements as well. In my view the second example tells the reader everything he needs to know while the first one, although defining the attitude of Reid and the ward sister with extra words, actually diminishes the total effect. The lesson, of course, is that good dialogue, like good narrative, should always be kept sparse and pruned.

GAGGING THE AUTHOR

The one 'voice' that should never appear in the dialogue is the author's. How does the beginner avoid the temptation to throw in his own pet theories and beliefs?

If he is a person of strong beliefs, it is doubtful that he will be able to. In fact, it is possible that one of his reasons for writing is to dramatise those beliefs. However, it is imperative that he does not seem to be proselytising, or he might offend or irritate the reader.

The method he must use is the one discussed earlier. He must use his characters to defend or advance his theories or beliefs and they must do it subtly and sympathetically. On no account must the reader feel he is being preached to. To avoid this happening, characters who have opposite views should play an important role in his novel and also be allowed to express their views. It is the weighing of one case against the other that should swing the argument in the writer's favour, but it must be done fairly or the writer might damage his case rather than promote it. A highly important factor in achieving this end is the depth of the characterisation. The writer must define his characters from the very beginning, give them their roles, and then make certain their behaviour is consistent throughout the story. In this way he will get over his viewpoints without seeming to intrude himself.

SPOKEN ALOUD

Dialogue, although written on the page, is essentially for the inner ear. Are there any advantages in reading it aloud?

Not very many. I think the mention of 'inner ear' is the clue here.

Although it can sometimes help to read one's dialogue aloud to check for false notes and inconsistency, it is, as I stated earlier, a fact that dialogue written for a novel is not the same as dialogue written specifically to be spoken aloud, as in a play. For the latter, reading aloud is almost essential. For a novel, dialogue that seems perfectly natural when scanned by the eye often can seem slightly stiff and literary when read aloud.

The reason, I feel, is because the ear translates speech differently to the eye. The ear is used to hearing badly-spoken and mutilated language and can pick out the few grains of wheat from the cartloads of chaff. The eye is not used to this jumble and so needs a better use of the language to make sense of it. This is precisely why I advised the beginner not to use much dialect in his conversations. His ear will understand it but his eye will be baffled by the grotesque spelling necessary to convey its meaning.

Dialogue in novels, therefore, has to be somewhat more literary than dialogue in plays so as to convey its meaning, and yet it must *seem* natural. It is this difference that causes novices a great deal of trouble. It will help a beginner to study the dialogue of first class authors. See how perfectly natural their written conversations seem on paper and yet how subtly different those conversations seem when read aloud. This difference in technique needs to be mastered before one can become a good novelist.

ILLUSTRATION 10: Which voice is which?

An individual and recognisable speech pattern for each character is essential for reader involvement.

Characteristics shouldn't be overdone, but it is essential that the author 'hears' the voices.

Who	character	type of voice	
Mary	30s Ordinary sensitive	Straightforward sense of composure	*Underlying anxiousness Strain shows*
James	Artistic/highly strung	Nervous, quick to anger	*Sraccato speech in musical rhythm*
Mother	Ferocious and domineering *—but well mannered*	Strong, demanding of others *Speaks her mind. Talks in clipped 'upper class' accent*	
Ethel	Vinegarish *Very sharp tongued*	Demonstrates the air of disappointment with her life and marriage. *Jealousy permeates everything*	
Frank	Eager, anxious to please	The peacemaker, quick nervous manner	
Stella	Lively, maybe flighty, not a local	Bright and flippant *'Bright young thing' Devil may care tones must mask a deep sadness*	
Gwen	Half sister to Stella	Welsh — or with a slight hint in syntax	
Mervyn	Brash and flash	Air of used car salesman Slick, wheedling. *Barrow boy spiel*	
Doctor	Neat, country type	Professional air and a bedside manner reassuring	

NOTE: Dialogue will play a large part in revelation of states of mind and action. Build tension into statements. Actions may not match words, as characters are all playing out a part behind a mask of propriety or self-interest. Dialect won't be necessary, (wouldn't add anything) given the middle-class, fairly wealthy situation of the English family, even though in south west setting.

11 Taste

One very important ingredient in a book would seem to be taste, a quality which is apparent in all your novels. Do you see this as an essential element of dramatic work?

Taste in dramatic work, knowing how much to say and how much to leave out, is very important. In a novel you meet it in all guises, not to overwrite a scene, not to make a character too good or too bad, not to make a scene too horrific, and so on. It is sometimes a very delicate tightrope and none of us can claim we haven't fallen off it at one time or another.

What some beginners do not appreciate is that occasionally the writer needs to understate to be believed. I once had to write about a major operation and obtained permission to see one. To my disbelief blood appeared on the arc lights during the next few hours. Had I put that in my story, people would have put their noses in the air and said it was a writer's imagination at work.

The same applies to war autobiographies, to cases of abused children, to tortured political prisoners, and many other examples of man's inhumanity to man. Sometimes the facts are more bizarre or horrific than the general public is capable of believing and in such cases one has either to dilute them or leave them out altogether.

Can such judgement be taught or is it instinctive?

I tend to think some of it is instinctive. The problem is, of course, that we are writing for all kinds of people, all with different emotional thresholds. Therefore we can only use ourselves as guinea pigs, which means some people will find our work either too explicit or not explicit enough. As there is absolutely nothing one can do about this, we can only continue to make our own subjective judgements. Perhaps this might explain why some novelists are more popular than others - perhaps their personal tastes are more in tune with the public common denominator. That's a possibility to ponder over!

THE USE OF EXPLICIT SEX

The use of explicit sex is a controversial aspect of modern novels. As some of your novels contain very powerful, but non-explicit sexual scenes, what are your views on this modern trend?

Far too many writers have used and still are using sex to titillate and encourage the reader to read on, which is a tacit admission the book's construction is faulty. If a book is well assembled and well written there is no need for this. Sex is as legitimate an element of a novel as any other aspect of life, but should be used only when it adds depth to the story or is the subject of the story itself. In these cases there should be no coyness in its use. But to use it only as titillation is to confess to a lack of skill and a lack of taste.

I've heard you say that we are explicit today because we have lost the art of being erotic. What exactly do you mean by this?

I believe it has happened because of the very freedom the sexual revolution has given us. When I began writing in the Fifties, explicit sex wasn't allowed, so one had to devise ways of putting images into the reader's mind by inference. Ironically this was very effective for the same reason that a man or woman will create a fantasy counterpart if a writer gives them the opportunity. The love scene they will create will be their ideal love scene and the behaviour of the lover will match their fantasies.

This is not possible when graphic descriptions are given. If every grisly detail is furnished, the reader becomes a voyeur, not a participant, and so his pleasure is often reduced accordingly. This is why sex scenes in films or on television arouse so much antipathy or contempt. In their freedom, the writers and directors have forgotten, or never learned, that eroticism is subjective and personal, and the sexual acts of others often appear crude or ludicrous to normal men and women.

I believe graphic descriptions have brought about another loss too, although one less easy to define. Before the Sixties there was an invisible frame or boundary around erotic scenes which a writer was not allowed to cross. Consequently he had to refine and refine again his words to gain the maximum effect possible. In doing this he packed energy into the frame like steam being compressed inside a boiler.

But today there is no frame and so no compressed energy. A writer has no need to learn the skills of sexual symbolism but even if the skill were there, the lack of a restraining frame would dissipate its effect. Perhaps it is a classic example of the need to handle freedom with restraint and good taste.

TITLES

Of Immense Importance

Is a good title essential and if so, should the writer have it firmly in mind when starting the novel?

Titles are very important. Some authors and publishers contend a good one can upturn sales by 40 or even 50 per cent and I wouldn't disagree with them.

It is true that sometimes a writer is lucky enough to have a title before he starts the book. Sometimes a few graphic words can 'grab' him so much that he creates 100,000 words from them. That is possibly the ideal title because the entire work is tailored to it.

But that is a relatively rare occurrence. In most cases the writer is worrying about, or at least thinking about, the title during the process of writing the book. Sometimes he will find a striking one from his own prose and because it is linked with his story, it will be well suited to it. Or he might decide that one of his characters might make a good title. Or a place name in the story might be suitable. Or a quirky phrase. The choice, fortunately, is very wide.

If a writer is held up for a good title, there are always quotations to fall back on. The Bible, Shakespeare, and the Psalms have provided rich pickings for hundreds of writers. A Dictionary of Quotations and Proverbs is another rich source, as are the works of poets.

On the other hand there are authors who don't find a title until after they have finished their book. This is irritating because very often one can't get the story off to the publisher until one is found. At the same time, a writer can't hurry and be slipshod over his choice because, as we have said, titles are important.

Style and Length

Which is best, the slick and clever title or the solemn; the long or the short?

Regarding types of title, alliterative ones are quite popular because they roll easily off the tongue. Chu Chin Chow is an excellent example. Although a title's aptness to its subject is more important than alliteration, nevertheless a combination of the two makes a title even better.

Regarding length, most publishers dislike long titles on two counts. One, because it's usually difficult for the reader to remember it; two, because it's hard to print it on the spine of the jacket unless it is very small, which isn't to the author's advantage.

Inspiration

Have you ever found yourself without a title, and growing desperate?

Yes, it happened to me with the second novel of my Yorkshire trilogy. After I finished it, a month passed without my thinking of a good title and I was growing impatient because the book was commissioned and the deadline date was near. Then I had to attend a funeral - not of someone close to me, let me hastily add - and I was lustily singing the 23rd psalm when my eyes spotted a line in the third verse - IN PRESENCE OF MY FOES. I felt very excited because it was the perfect title for the book, and it was only when the singing stopped that I remembered where I was and what I should be thinking about. It's a shameful confession but I'm afraid that's the way we authors are. We have a built-in recorder that sometimes seems to take control of us. Perhaps, however, that is something we should admit only to ourselves.

You used very strong titles for those three Yorkshire novels, didn't you? I'm thinking of the other two as well, RAGE OF THE INNOCENT and YEARS OF THE FURY. Are you in favour of strong titles for all books?

I think it's a case of horses for courses. If a novelist is writing a gentle novel of an old couple set in an idyllic setting, then a soft title like On Golden Pond would be more suitable. Like many other aspects of writing, balance and taste are so important.

Uniquely Yours

There is no copyright on titles but it is obviously to an author's advantage to choose one that is unique and not open to confusion with a similarly titled work. Is there a way of ensuring this?

It isn't easy and I doubt if there is any way to be absolutely certain one's title hasn't been used before. But titles currently in use can be checked from Books in Print which most libraries stock and there are reference books listing older works.

If a similar title is found, then the writer must decide for himself how serious the clash is. If the book is long dead and the writer is in love with his title, then perhaps the similarity does not matter. If a book has been published recently with the same title, however, then the writer would be wise to make a change.

ILLUSTRATION 11: What to leave out, and choosing its title

In a book dealing with the sensitive subject of madness care has to be taken not to weaken the theme or to alienate the reader with over-emphasis on graphic details.

Possibilities:

James' increasing madness

What form? — *not at first, but increasing.*
Is it violent?

Repression Sexual overtones? — *the reverse, (it's sex guilt)*

The adultery ← *This was a one-off, compounded by finding out it's his sister-in-law* → James & Stella

Flashback to affair?

Explicit — to dramatize his guilt **NO** — *that would detract from idea it's in his mind*

Stella & Mervyn

Highlight sex
Is there sex?

Doctor

(though Ethel sees and misinterprets — naturally!)

In love with Mary **Yes. Very restrained, doesn't declare it.**
Flirtatious hints?
Professional — but!

A good title should reflect the tone and story-line of the book. Choosing one can be a long process of elimination.

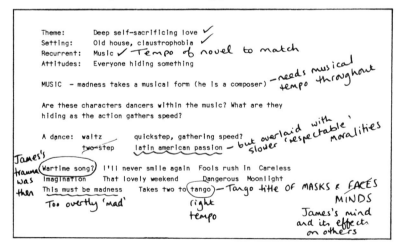

Theme: Deep self-sacrificing love ✓
Setting: Old house, claustrophobia ✓
Recurrent: Music ✓ *Tempo of novel to match*
Attitudes: Everyone hiding something

MUSIC — madness takes a musical form (he is a composer) — *needs musical tempo throughout*

Are these characters dancers within the music? What are they hiding as the action gathers speed?

A dance: waltz   quickstep, gathering speed? — *but overlaid with 'respectable' moralities*
two-step   latin american passion — *slower*

James's trauma was then (Wartime song?) I'll never smile again Fools rush in Careless
Imagination   That lovely weekend   Dangerous Moonlight
This must be madness   Takes two to (tango) — *Tango title* OF MASKS & FACES
Too overtly 'mad'   *right tempo*   MINDS
James's mind and its effects on others

12 Style

Style is the dress of thought or, alternatively, the man himself, according to 18th century sources. How do you define style in literature?

Style is simply the way one writes. A non-literary person would probably be surprised to hear that authors write as differently as they talk or gesticulate, but they do and in time we are all recognised by our style.

Although writing technique and the correct usage of the English language can be taught, style cannot. It evolves from the author himself and perhaps has a bearing on his own personality.

Style takes time to evolve, however, because in the beginning we tend to over-write, to use too many adjectives, adverbs, and flowery phrases. I know I did and think it is a common fault with us all. We are so keen to get our meaning over that we overplay our hand.

DRESSING DOWN

Are you, therefore, advocating simple writing rather than the florid?

Most definitely. The truth is that the prose of almost any amateur writer, however talented, can be improved by cutting, perhaps as much as forty per cent. If he goes through one of his earlier works carefully, he will see what I mean. He will find firstly that half to two thirds of its adjectives and adverbs can be eliminated. Then he should look to see if he has said the same thing twice in a different way. If he has, he should eliminate one or the other because it is a recognised fact that readers need to be told a thing only once and they will remember it.

The writer should also see if he has used a long word when a short one would do equally well. He should cut and cut again until he will begin to see the real flower instead of the leaves around it. He should always aim for simplicity and he should remember what I said earlier: that it is wise to leave some things to the reader's imagination. Writing and reading are complementary pursuits and the reader will get far more from a book if he has to use his own mind too.

Another quality that defines an author's style is his use of similes and/or word pictures. These are verbal comparisons to heighten the description of some object or action. Authors who see their novel in vision as they write it are perhaps better with these analogies than those who think entirely in words, although I've no doubt the latter authors will dispute this. Certainly all authors should strive to develop this skill because it adds a vivid quality to one's work as well as establishing one's own particular style.

STYLE v SALES

At the same time, as with so many other aspects of writing, a writer shouldn't be deceived into thinking that a good style necessarily equates with good sales. The public will forgive (even if they notice) poor grammar and syntax if the story-line keeps them on the edge of their seats. In his time writers like Peter Cheney proved this and plenty of others have followed him down that broad highway since.

But if a writer has the ambition to be both a stylist and a superb story-teller, there is in my opinion no better author to study than Somerset Maugham who, with his concise, incisive prose, proved that quality writing and popularity *can* go hand in hand.

To recap, be ruthless with one's work. Cut out every unnecessary word. Polish grammar and punctuation and sharpen dialogue. Use word pictures to illustrate important incidents but don't overdo it or the prose will become flowery and artificial. Do all this without losing the initial spontaneity of the idea, and soon a style will emerge that will be the writer's personal hallmark.

TONE AND APPROACH

Being consistent throughout the novel - in other words maintaining a level tone - is an important stylistic aim. Should tone vary according to the readership at which the novel is aimed?

Rather sadly, I feel it must. For example, clichés are quite popular in the mass market as they make for easier reading. Similarly, a popular thriller using literary language would not please the general public who want a paperback to read on the beach and then throw away.

The same applies to women's romantic fiction or teenage novels whose readers expect a 'streetwise' image with which they can identify. In these books and others of their kind one is forced to consider the readership when planning the novel and to pitch the tone and style to suit it. It is then vital to keep those elements consistent throughout the entire work.

How far does the material determine the style? For example, THE TORMENTED, a hard-hitting 'masculine' novel about revolution must have had a very different approach to your novel, THE WIDER SEA OF LOVE, told through a woman's eyes?

In certain types of women's fiction a softer style is necessary in a story about women and their emotions because in general they do not think or speak the same way as men (although some would say the gap is fast narrowing). One can't be specific about these items because they depend so much on the characters and the story themselves but commonsense will take care of most of them.

Yet, while allowing for these provisions, there should be no easing up with the *tightness* of a story. Everything said earlier about the need to keep one's prose sharp and clean is just as applicable if a story is seen through the eyes of a woman as of a man. The style might be softer but the image should be equally uncluttered with unnecessary verbiage.

HUMOUR

Should humour be used in a serious work? Or will it detract from the essential solemnity of the theme?

No. If used properly, humour will highlight a dramatic theme for the very reason that light delineates shade and vice versa. Or, to put it in a more pungent way: *wisdom without wit is like polish without spit.* At the same time humour should never be forced into the story for its own sake. It should always emerge naturally, as in the example below.

"Shock waves are greatly magnified in effect when they enter solids like earth or rock - they become tremendously destructive. Normally the blast from a surface bomb goes upwards where it is wasted. But in this case the shock waves from your bombs will go upwards into this mountain overhang and shiver up the fissure like a seismic disturbance.

"Our scientists haven't been able to calculate exactly how many bombs it will take but they are confident that a succession of explosions will fracture that fissure more and more until the front part of the overhang comes crashing down. To put it inaccurately but graphically, the shock punch from your bombs will throw old Trolljell's head backwards, his neck will snap like a carrot, and another redskin will bite the dust."

(633 Squadron)

This is an extract from the Air Commodore's speech when he is briefing the aircrews on the highly dangerous mission they are soon to undertake. I've used the example from a war novel because those who have served in the Forces will know how frequently humour was and is used during briefings to disguise the seriousness of an operation. It is highly effective because it relaxes the nerves of listening men.

DON'T FORCE THE LAUGHS

*You say humour shouldn't be forced into a story for its own sake.
Isn't it also true that it shouldn't be forced into the author?*

I agree. We've all met people who are hopeless at telling jokes and
it can be excruciating having to listen to them. The same thing
applies to writers. If a man knows he's not a natural humorist -
and he ought to know this before he steps into long trousers - then
he shouldn't try to inject jokes into his story or, even worse, invent
them. He must produce his humour by inventing situations in his
novel that are funny in themselves. This can be very effective and
most writers are capable of inventing such situations. Those that
can't should keep their eyes and ears open, because funny incidents
are happening all around them.

Used well, humour is effective in almost any aspect of life. Emotionally we are frail creatures who sometimes find our tragedies too
much to bear. At such times our own pysche often comes to our
aid and in the middle of our grief we might suddenly have a
humorous thought. Highly-strung people are more prone to this
experience than others and because of their sensitivity it often
makes them feel guilty.

It should not. It has only been their self-protective mechanism
coming to their aid. An author writing about such a person could
therefore give him such a thought in a moment of grief and, if
done with skill, it can be most effective.

Equally a friend, seeing a comrade in distress, will often help him
with a joke. These are usually mordant jokes but no less effective
for that. A writer should use humour in these ways, remembering
always that drama is emotion and emotion needs contrast or it will
become too heavy and sate its audience.

*This kind of humour would come into the category of black
comedy, wouldn't it? In your two books SAFFRON'S WAR and
SAFFRON'S ARMY, service jokes play a big part.*

I suppose many service jokes do come under that category. But
your mention of these two books reminds me of another way of
producing humour, by the clash of disparate personalities. Saffron is an eager beaver while his wartime colleague Bickers is a
scrounger who doesn't see why he should risk his life for England's
Lord Norfolks and Lord Salisburys. The clash of personalities with
viewpoints as different as this can create all kinds of comical
situations and dialogue.

Would you, then, call these two books black comedies?

Not entirely. I see black comedies as macabre comedies. Some of
the jokes and situations in these books might be black but not all
of them. Perhaps black-and-white comedies might describe them
better.

CLICHÉS

Avoid clichés, that's the advice given to would-be writers. Is the use of stock phrases a sign of mental laziness, or are there times when such use is justified?

This is a problem every writer must face. Told by the pundits he must avoid clichés, he will have no problem in his early days because he will have his own individual way of saying things. The problem begins after his third or fourth book. By this time his special way of saying things has made his own clichés and he can't continue to use them without his editor and his readers noticing.

It is also why, contrary to popular belief, novels do not get any easier to write as a writer's published work increases. In fact they can become harder as the author struggles to find new ways of saying things. I am, however, talking about novelists who care about their language and are writing for a certain segment of the public. Some popular novels and serials do not demand such care: indeed there is a theory that their readership welcomes clichés because they make for easier reading. So if a writer is aiming down-market, he need not be so careful to leave out the 'sickening thuds' and 'heaving bosom' clichés that other novelists strive to avoid.

What you have just said applies to clichés of language. What are your views on the clichés of situations so often found in modern blockbuster novels?

To be absolutely frank, I'm not one who favours seducing the reader by fantasy stories about the rich and the powerful, although I accept that such books sell well. To me the formula has become stylized. They usually begin with the maid of a poor family being raped by the spoilt son of the local rich family and from then, until the wronged girl becomes fabulously rich herself and destroys her rivals, one can anticipate almost every situation before it happens. In other words the incidents themselves as well as the idea have become clichés.

At this point let me quickly say that I'm not suggesting we should look down our noses at this kind of literature. If a book or a serial, however clichéd or badly written, brings comfort to some old or bedridden person and brings them temporary forgetfulness from their loneliness or pain, who has the right to say the story is not serving as valuable a purpose as any masterpiece?

Nevertheless, as a well written book *ought* to be more entertaining than a badly written one if its author has paid care over its plotting, then one's advice must be to avoid clichés whenever possible.

ILLUSTRATION 12: Style v sales, or cleaving the cleavage

Where is the novel to be aimed? A clichéd and pop style may be the current vogue, but will it soon fade, dragging the novel into obscurity with it?

Will pandering to a popular genre unnecessarily restrict the expansive and reflective theme of the novel?

These are points to consider before pen touches paper.

What's currently popular?

Crime

Not deep enough — *& there's no crime (except an adulterous sex)*

Women's romance

Needs more sweetness
Too cloying in context — could lapse into melodrama

Thriller

Madness isn't thrilling
This is downbeat — the reverse of a rising thriller pace

Teenage behaviour

No teenagers

What is MASKS AND MINDS to be?

A psychological study *The effect on the protagonists*

Will it fit a genre slot? *No*

Nearest to thriller but not to be defined as such

Where is it aimed? *Unsuitable theme*

Mass market = slick and wordy writing, little characterisation
Cliches needed *won't fit this slot*

Straight novel — Literary audience?
Tight writing, strong on character study.

Humour?

Nothing conscious. — *But light relief in sub-plots*

Explicit sex in old affair?

Intrusive and not acceptable by censor
Definitely NO cleavage!

Would be unduly intrusive. The affair per se isn't important. James's state of mind is.

---

13   Conditions of Work

With all the elements needed for a novel taken into account, the novice can now begin the actual writing. I know that some writers need peace and their own office while others can write curled up in an armchair. What sort of work conditions do you advise for him? What conditions work best for you?

I'm not one of those people who believe a writer must be in some cosy garden house or ivory castle to write a masterpiece. I always remember visiting Kipling's one-time cottage on Devil's Peak near Cape Town and seeing the glorious view from its windows. It was given to Kipling by Rhodes who had this naive belief that beautiful surroundings are necessary to art. Rhodes was away from Cape Town for three months and when he returned and visited Kipling, he rubbed his hands in anticipation and asked to see the great writer's work. Somewhat irritably, Kipling showed him an empty notebook.

Rhodes looked astonished. "But why? Isn't the view beautiful enough for you?"

Kipling scowled. "Of course it's beautiful. It's so beautiful I couldn't do anything else but look at it."

There is truth in that. Beauty can distract as well as inspire. I believe that a determined writer can write under any conditions. I wrote my first five novels in a tiny attic full of discarded furniture and with an oil stove so old and smoky that it nearly destroyed my lungs.

Writing isn't a comfortable occupation as so many people think - perhaps it isn't meant to be. Didn't the novelist Lynne Reid Banks say: "If you love writing you must be an amateur - real pros all loathe it, grizzling continually about how hard, lonely and boring it is."

I agree with this completely. If I find myself too comfortable or happy I lie back and enjoy it. I don't spoil it by writing. Nor am I losing good work by doing this because I don't believe a contented mind lends itself to powerful literature. If that thought has depressing connotations, ask yourself how many people are truly contented. The answer tells us it isn't something we need worry about too much.

So conditions are unimportant, as long as you can discipline the mind to writing?

Yes, always provided the cat doesn't knock ink all over your papers or a screaming child doesn't smash your typewriter (although there are some of us who have overcome even those traumas). What matters far more is that one writes in the *same place* every day. If a writer does this, the effect over the weeks and months is to brainwash him. He will walk into his attic or cubby hole and the familiar sights, the cracked ceiling, the torn wallpaper, the shabby curtains, will click on his mental switch and he is away. He walks out so many hours later and his switch turns off.

You don't agree, obviously, that a writer has to wait for the Muse of Inspiration before being able to put pen to paper?

The truth, of course, is that there isn't a Muse. No professional believes in her or, even worse, relies on her. Inspiration is sweat and concentration. One sets one's conscious mind working and the hidden machinery behind it goes into action. The results might not come immediately, they might not come that day or the next, and that's why the amateur believes in inspiration. What really happens is that the subconscious mind has been working on one's problems since they were fed into the mental computer and quite suddenly, hey presto, it comes up with the answers. The importance of working in the same environment is that the familiar sights greatly speed up these processes. Association of ideas is the modern term for it.

Not that I'm saying the sight of a bat flitting around a moonlit belfry or a cormorant flying low over a crimson sea won't set one's fantasies and imagination at work, but that is quite a different thing from the sweat and blood of writing a novel. Here regular application is the secret. The same place every day and the same time if possible. Then a writer need not worry about the Muse. She'll respect his perseverance and play her full part.

Again, there is a dichotomy of views over writing production. Is it possible to set a 'so many words a day' target?

Trying to write the same number of words every day is the quickest way to a coronary that I know. One's health and mental activity vary quite considerably from day to day and, more importantly, so does one's imagination. One day a writer might produce only 700 words. (I'm not including here how many words were written down but only how many were kept!) The same might happen on the second day and even on the third and if he isn't experienced the writer might feel disappointed, even disheartened, that he has failed to meet an arbitrary target.

But then, for no apparent reason, he will write 2,500 good words on the fourth day which, if averaged out, means he has in effect written 1,150 words every day, which isn't a bad achievement.

This stop-go in terms of output will always happen no matter how detailed a synopsis a writer has constructed - as I said earlier, the creative part of writing is in the writing itself. If he had set himself so many words to write every day, he might have struggled on into the night and felt like a screwed-up rag the next morning. And still have produced only rubbish. Write for so many hours a day or night and don't worry about the number of words. The average per day will still come as a pleasant surprise.

What has happened, of course, is that the subconscious mind has been eliminating items it didn't need for the story or exploring new avenues for the story-line during those first three days. Once it has found the right way, it moves the story on with a large bound. Then it might pause again when it reaches another difficult part in the plot. And so on.

DELIBERATELY USING THE SUBCONSCIOUS

You have mentioned the subconscious. Is it really such a valuable tool, provided you can exercise it or train it?

I find it so. We've just seen how it works in the production process but that happens automatically. But it can also be called on consciously to give help.

For example, you are sitting at your desk struggling to create a sentence and however you switch round the words, the exact meaning you are trying to impart will not come. The minutes slip past and the sentence seems to grow clumsier rather than clearer. You start to shift about in your chair, you feel yourself growing hot and irritable, you begin to wonder what madness drove you even to think of writing anything as perverse and difficult as a novel.

The same thing can happen with a single word. You page through your thesaurus time and again and still you can't find that one single word that your sentence needs so badly. "What's the matter?" you ask yourself. "Why am I so stupid this morning? Am I burned out? Have I got Alzheimer's disease?"

We have all gone through these traumas. I'm sure I took years off my life in my early days, squirming about on my seat and hating the perverse world I lived in. I'd finish my stint for the day worn out and in a filthy mood.

It was, and is, so unnecessary. The answer couldn't be more simple. Give yourself a few minutes thinking about your problem so that it is firmly implanted in your mind. If the answer doesn't come then, don't worry. Rise from your seat, throw the problem out of the window, and go and make yourself a cup of coffee. Give yourself ten or fifteen minutes to drink it and then return leisurely to your desk. And in nine cases out of ten you'll find you have the exact sentence or word you were so desperately searching for.

14 Writing the Novel from the Synopsis

THERE'S A BEGINNING . . .

With the writer in his chosen place of work and the synopsis before him, what should be his first thought before he begins writing the novel?

His first thought should be the immediate introduction of his main characters. If he has structured his synopsis correctly, the incident or situation to do this will be present. If it is not, he must create one. This will prove relatively easy if he has decided to write in the 1st person because the narrator, one of the main characters, is involved from the first words that are used. If he has chosen the 3rd person, however - and if he is a beginner he would be wise to make this choice - then he should introduce his hero or heroine in the opening paragraphs and his villain not far behind.

What about these opening paragraphs? Do you like 'big' ones or more muted ones?

Writers have been told many times to open with what I call the BIG BANG theory, that is to open with a dramatic paragraph that captures a reader immediately and drags him head over heels into the action.

It is true that the first paragraph is important, particularly if you aren't yet a well-known author. However, I personally prefer the more muted approach.

Will you give a few examples from your novels?

The first one is from a thriller.

> *I noticed her the moment I topped the grassy dune that separated the beach from the road. She was standing on one of the beach fortifications; her poised figure, silhouetted against the fading sky, making me think of a wild animal that had been suddenly alerted.*

> (The Devil Behind Me)

The second deals with the conflicts between sex and love.

> *Sarah Ashley was never certain why she turned off the main Bere Regis - Bournemouth road that late November afternoon. The lane that ran through the Great Heath and the Forest to Wareham would lengthen, not shorten, her journey home, and later she would put the impulse down only to her enjoyment of driving her car in bad weather. Grey mist settling in rime on gorse and hedgerows, wind soughing across the fields, winter darkness closing in fast: these things always made the tiny world of Sarah Ashley's car seem oddly snug and attractive.*

(The Wider Sea of Love)

The third is from the first book of the trilogy loosely based on the lives of my parents.

> *The boy, half hidden in the hedge, was sitting very still. Even when a fly landed on his forehead, he did not stir. Only his eyes moved. They were playing back and forth across a field of young corn that lay like a sunlit lake before him.*
>
> *The fly moved down to his nose. He grimaced and the insect flew away. The hum of summer pervaded the silence. With the sun a glowing cauldron above and the tall trees motionless, time seemed as hushed and expectant as the boy himself.*

(Rage of the Innocent)

The first example, being from a thriller, is meant to hint the girl is afraid, although of what the observer does not yet know. This provides the element of mystery. The mention of fortifications is also deliberate because of the word's connotation with aggression or violence.

The second example, needing a lower key opening, uses the woman's decision to take an alternative route home to suggest drama to come. It also uses weather to create atmosphere and so promote the same purpose. Although the latter is deliberately played down by the woman's thoughts, the reader is not deceived and knows fate is about to intervene in her life. What that intervention is to be provides the mystery.

The third example also uses weather and atmosphere to create effect, although in entirely the opposite way to the second example. Here it is a perfect summer day, which makes the boy's behaviour the more mysterious. In a way it is almost deliberately down key but it does possess one key word, *expectant* which provides the element of mystery. Nothing more is needed to move the story on.

It will be noticed that in all cases the main character in the story is introduced immediately. In the case of THE DEVIL BEHIND ME, because it is written in the first person, it contains two characters, the girl and the narrator.

To recap, opening paragraphs should introduce the major characters and by their style and careful use of words set the general mood of the novel. As many would-be readers scan opening paragraphs before committing themselves to a novel, it is obvious they should be carefully and thoughtfully written.

I'm aware that some writers prefer a more dramatic approach but as we discussed earlier, such openings can cause an imbalance in plot structure. If one begins with high action, there is for a while an almost inevitable decline in tension: indeed one might have pre-empted one's first mini-crisis. In other words the graph of drama is distorted.

The action-packed opening also affects the writer emotionally. Conscious he must keep up the excitement, he can easily fall into the trap of trying too hard to sustain it. This will not only distort the plot structure but paradoxically will be counterproductive in its effect on the reader. There is a high watermark of emotion in us all and if we are fed with too much excitement we will lose the ability to respond to it.

But you have opened with some pretty powerful paragraphs in novels such as the 633 SQUADRON series, haven't you?

Books of extreme violence, like war novels, are possible exceptions. Readers of these books expect high action and are geared to receive it. Moreover, because there is so much action available, one can get away with a violent scene and still be able to cap it later.

Even so I believe the opening paragraph should have a direct bearing on the theme and not be there for violence's sake. Let me give an example.

> *The 21cm rocket struck the B.17 full on its starboard inner engine. The explosion was followed by a ball of black smoke. A few seconds later the wing sheared away and the Fortress began spinning earthward. Three parachutes blossomed out into the tracer-streaked sky. With seven men still trapped inside, the B.17 disappeared into the clouds that hid the earth.*

(Operation Crucible)

Action, yes, but with a purpose. The novel, set in 1943, is built round the American complaint that their heavy bombers were not being given adequate protection by the RAF and continues with the subsequent efforts by the British to nail this criticism. Here I suggest it is justifiable to begin with a battle scene because it gives an apparent cause for the American complaint that is to follow. And, of course, the subject lends itself to action scenes that can easily match the opening paragraphs.

Your novel THE STORM KNIGHT began in a totally different way and broke all the general rules you gave earlier by not mentioning a single main character on the first page? Why that format?

There is another kind of opening which becomes necessary when factors other than the main characters play a leading part in a story. That novel begins as follows:

My first sight of that fjord was like a blow in the face. I'd seen impressive mountain scenery before, both in the Alps and back home in Canada, but this had an almost sinister quality. The southern mountain guarding its entrance was obscenely ugly, a rotund colossus whose summit was still capped with snow and whose black belly rolled slowly over until it plunged downwards. The fjord itself was in the shadow of storm clouds and approaching night but the snowy peaks were crimsoned by the dying sun, and the effect of shadow on storm-light was Valkyrian.

(The Storm Knight)

The reason the breathtaking scenery of Norway opens the novel is because it plays a major part in the story. It is, so to speak, a character in its own right, so it is introduced early as major characters should be. Its Valkyrian description is to suggest its role in the story will be sinister rather than beneficial.

However, another character does appear with it in this opening paragraph. Because the novel is written in the first person, it introduces one of its three main human characters, the narrator.

Once again there is a case of horses for courses here but war novels and unusual novels apart, I prefer the more muted but intriguing opening with each succeeding chapter tightening the screw.

. . . AND A MIDDLE . . .

At this point the novel is well under way, and the author must now move on to the next stage. How is he to make sure the reader keeps on reading?

This is the point at which all the 'ingredients' so far discussed come together to be mixed into the 'cake'. From this point on he has to lead his reader into a journey of imagination and discovery.

Although all the ingredients will be used in the progression of his story, their proportion will depend to a considerable extent on the nature of that story. If the writer has chosen a thriller or an action-packed novel, he will make extensive use of conflict and suspense, and in general his dialogue will be brief and to the point. He will use a fast tempo and its pace will quicken as he nears the end of his story, rather like a runner seeing the tape ahead of him and sprinting towards it.

In stories of detection, the mix changes. Although conflict and suspense will still be utilised, the mystery of 'who dun it' will be the dominant factor.

In gentler themes, the tempo can be slower. Now the emphasis is on character, dialogue, and atmosphere. Suspense and conflict will still be present but they might now take the forms of indecision and self-doubts.

In philosophical works, the mix changes again. Inner conflicts and dialogue might dominate, along with powerful characterisation. Suspense will still be present but its form might now lie in the resolution or non-resolution of ideas or beliefs.

One can only give broad guidelines because, even within the same genre, the proportion of the mix will vary according to the story-line the writer has constructed. For this reason he should give careful thought to them as his novel progresses.

I'm often asked 'how long should a book be and how many chapters should it have?' I tell pupils the story-line dictates both. But should chapters be long or short? And should chapter-end hooks be used to tantalise?

You are quite right. There is no standard length for a novel. Certain themes need greater development than others, and a writer usually discovers this as his work progresses. If a book seems to be going on and on, my advice to a writer is not to worry but to go ahead and finish it.

Nevertheless, although exceptions prove the rule, it is generally true that thrillers and crime novels are better books when their length is kept short, probably because a reader's interest, as well as his credulity, can be put under strain if demanded for too long. The same applies to love stories. If the poor man is kept waiting too long before he can embrace his beloved, his eye might well be tempted to stray elsewhere.

Regarding the number of chapters, this has much to do with a writer's personal style, as well as the construction of his story. Some scenes take longer to describe than others, and so chapter lengths will vary. There are no hard and fast rules here, provided the writer ends one chapter in a way that makes his reader want to move to the next one. Indeed, a book with chapters of equal length would look odd and artificial.

These devices that give a reader the desire to read on are sometimes called chapter-end hooks. Although in thrillers and their like they are more obvious than in so-called straight novels, they do appear in all novels although their form can be very subtle. One simple but effective way is to divide a scene or incident into two or even three chapters, which almost compels a reader to keep turning over the pages.

If the pace doesn't seem quite right, or the story isn't hanging together as well as the author would like, does he go back and keep re-writing the earlier chapters or does he keep going regardless?

He keeps going. The more he pauses to retrace his steps and to polish what he has written, the less likelihood there is of him ever finishing the book. The time to look back, to prune and re-shape, is when the first draft is finished. At this point the author knows his initial idea has proved itself as the inspiration for a full length novel, and he can now face the task of editing with confidence and enthusiasm.

There is another reason for keeping going until the end. When a writer is able to read his work straight through, he is better able to see it in proportion and to decide what is necessary and what isn't. He is also able to identify pages where he has been repetitive. By doing his pruning and editing at this stage, he will achieve a better balanced novel than if he had made his judgements earlier.

. . . AND AN ENDING

The end is in sight. The reader is anxious to get there. What devices speed up that process?

A writer's first concern should be to know when to end his novel. Denouements should never be lengthy. If irrelevant facts are fed into the story after its natural length, an anti-climax will be produced and all the work that has been put in earlier might be wasted.

Regarding ways of speeding up the ending, two devices can be used. One is to speed up the general tempo which can be done by the writing and by shortening paragraphs. A second method is to shorten the chapters. The effects can be compared with the yellow hatchings at the approach to a road junction, which give a motorist the illusion of speed.

HAPPY OR UNHAPPY ENDINGS

What are your feelings about happy and unhappy endings? There seems little doubt which the public prefer.

No one can advise a writer without seeing a detailed synopsis of his book and even then the way it is written might bring about a total change of mind. Most people do like happy endings, particularly those who read romantic stories. But what people like and what they get depends a great deal on the personality of the author. If he has a strong feeling for his novel, then he must give it the ending he believes it needs, no matter where the public preference lies. By the time he is two thirds of the way through his novel, his instincts will give him the answer and he should obey them. Certainly an unhappy ending will not kill a good book, as the novel Dr Zhivago proved. A sadder ending would be difficult to imagine and yet the novel was a world best-seller.

So my advice here is to obey one's instincts and have the ending that one feels gives the book its greater power.

15   Fiction from Fact

So far we have covered the elements and the problems in writing a normal book of fiction. But there is another kind of novel in which fact and fiction interlace. We touched on it briefly when discussing your 633 SQUADRON novels but as it is used very often in novels today, what is your definition of 'faction' as it is called?

It's a work in which an author takes a period of history, distinguished or notorious (like Beethoven's life, Napoleon's Thousand Days, or President Kennedy's assassination) and weaves his own characters and possibly, but not necessarily, his own plot into it.

ADVANTAGES OF FACTION

What are the advantages of using what can be a fairly restrictive format?

It adds verisimilitude to a fictitious work by its mention of characters and/or facts the reader already knows. Although these elements might not play a decisive part in the story, their very appearance gives a reader the sense he is staring through a window into history. This all adds to the entertainment value of the novel.

On a more serious level, faction also provides a very effective way of promoting or attacking a cause. As I've already maintained, few people have their minds changed by direct argument, however reasonable that argument might be. Their minds are usually made up beforehand and with their defences ready, they find it relatively easy to drive off all frontal attacks.

But are they ready for the attack from the rear? To change the metaphor, although they have all the doors locked, have they remembered the back room windows?

Remember always that a novelist is dealing with emotion. If he writes his novel well enough for its characters to win sympathy, a reader can easily forget the theme of the novel in his concern for the welfare of those characters. In this way a reader can be influenced into sympathising with a cause or an idea he previously rejected. The defiant head has been by-passed and the more vulnerable heart has been invaded instead. Dickens, of course, was a master of this.

But surely fiction alone can do this. So why use faction which is more difficult to handle?

Because of the way the introduction of real-life characters adds verisimilitude to the story-line. People who might otherwise say 'it's only fiction' are often seduced by the real names and places mentioned and so more likely to be influenced by the case the author is making.

Another advantage of faction is that sometimes it is the only way that truth can be told. This is particularly true if the book deals with very recent history. When I wrote 633 SQUADRON in 1954 the war had only been over for nine years, and as I had drawn some of my characters from men I had known, I could not use real names and a real locale without causing distress or even libel actions. I couldn't, for example, say that Squadron-Leader X was having an affair on the Station while his wife lived unsuspectingly in the nearby village. Or that Pilot Officer Z was a rank coward whose actions were endangering the lives of his fellow pilots. But I could say it in fiction. In other words - and this might come as a surprise to those who look down their noses at certain fictional works - some can tell the truth more truthfully than so-called factual books.

If one takes this on a national or international level, are you saying that faction might do things for history that a text book can't do?

It certainly can in terms of readability. People who never read text books will often pick up a work of drama, and if it is well researched and well written, they might develop an interest in history that was totally lacking before.

But occasionally the benefits go deeper than that. Faction might help to explain the motives of some historical characters. After all, a considerable amount of history is conjecture and an imaginative novelist has at least as good a chance of guessing the thoughts and intentions of a long-dead figure as an historian, always provided he has done his research thoroughly. Rightly or wrongly, artists are considered to have a higher level of intuition than their fellow men.

Can you give any other advantages of faction?

Faction can also be used to suggest what a real person's feelings or motives might have been *without making the actual claim* - in other words, by inference. While we all know that people are not always aware why they do this or that, there are cases where a writer, no matter how imaginative, might feel it presumptuous to declare unequivocally he knows the precise reason for those actions.

We've all seen these presumptions made, sometimes only to appeal to modern obsessions. A short story of Henry James, that was adapted into a television play, comes to mind. It was one of my favourite stories, being beautifully atmospheric and creepy, but the playwright gave it homosexual undertones that I felt were both false and unnecessary. The comments that followed - although I admit one is never sure whether they came from the playwright himself or from the press - were that these underlying influences were guiding James's pen when he wrote the story but he wasn't aware of them.

Now I think this was carrying intuitive guesswork too far because its inferences were questioning James' entire personality and character. At the same time, one would be perfectly entitled to create the work of a fictitious person very similar in personality and background to James and ascribe to him whatever motives and motivations one wanted within the context of the story-line. Whether readers then decide they are relative to James is up to them. In other words, the inference is there but presumption is not inflicted on a reader. The work can still stand on its two feet without it.

But can you call this faction?

Yes, I think one can because although the main character or characters may be fictitious, one can introduce many of the real-life factors that the original person came into contact with. This means the novel retains the verisimilitude that faction provides.

Is this what you did in your two novels A MEETING OF STARS and A CLASH OF STARS? The story-line does seem to have echoes of Amy Johnson's life?

Yes, the books were loosely based on her. There are some aspects of her personality that her own writings do not clarify, and the character of my heroine, Delia Summers, might perhaps fill those gaps. I say *might,* however, because the attempt to explain the inner workings of a person's mind can never be anything else but guesswork.

Yet another advantage of faction is to remind in dramatic form what the religious, political, or social conditions were like at a certain time. This is something I definitely set out to do in these two STARS books. To understand Amy Johnson's depressions, and her occasional breakdowns in health, one has to understand the enormous interest in flying that existed in the 1920s and 1930s. Present day pop stars receive nothing of the frenzied adoration these pioneer fliers received, and I have tried throughout the two books to illustrate the pressure of this and its effect on my heroine and on her marriage.

Of course my novels do not follow the exact story-line of Amy Johnson's life. If I had done that, readers would have had no need to buy or read the book. In my novels the heroine marries an American pilot and their love life is somewhat different in its development to Amy Johnson's marriage to Jim Mollison. Nevertheless my characters do fly to America together, as did the Mollisons; they receive the same frenzied reception over there; their private life is equally turbulent; and they do take part in the famous 1934 England to Australia Air Race.

What of the practice of using some other author's character as a basis for one's own series of novels?

I don't think much of the practice, not even if the writer has been given permission from the author's estate. It seems to me that if a so-called writer can't invent his own characters, he might be better employed in a profession less demanding on the imagination.

THE PITFALLS OF FACTION

Isn't there a danger, when writing about the past, of changing a historical character's motives to suit one's story-line?

There is indeed. A writer should only make such assumptions about historical figures whose motives have remained controversial over the years. Not of historical figures whose motives are known and documented. To twist the latter's intentions and deeds to suit one's story-line is to admit one can't invent a plot to contain them. It shows both a poverty of imagination and a poverty of ethics. Subjects of conjecture must be carefully chosen, and even then treated with discrimination and integrity.

From this I take it that you dislike the so-called character assassination?

I believe it is despicable to introduce some known figure, heroic or honourable, for the sole purpose of traducing them or giving unproven unsavoury reasons for their actions.

It is done, of course, because in our society today it is fashionable and profitable to knock the good or the valiant, and sadly some authors are doing this more and more as they find the practice is an aid to sales. They are also well aware they cannot be called to task by the dead.

A variation of this practice is to attribute to one's own countrymen the courageous deeds of foreigners. I remember seeing a film in which the British and the Americans destroyed the heavy water threat in Norway. As in reality this act was carried out entirely by Norwegians, many of whom are still alive and some of whom I'm proud to call my friends, the sight of the felony made me want to hurl something at the screen. One wonders what the Norwegians, who risked their lives on the operation, must have felt if the wretched film ever reached them.

Didn't you redress this in OPERATION VALKYRIE?

I tried. But the impact of films is so great that I'm certain millions of people believe what they saw on the screen. This despicable practice, done purely for profit, seems to be growing apace in books as well as in films and at times makes one ashamed of one's profession.

DISADVANTAGES OF FACTION

You stated earlier that faction was hard to write. What are its major disadvantages?

I've only found one disadvantage but as it involves writing difficulties, perhaps I can discuss the two points together.

If the writer does his work with integrity and keeps to the *known* facts of history, and it is my contention that he should, then faction is much, much harder to write than ordinary fiction because it loses its usual freedoms. In an ordinary novel, the growth of the story-line is organic: its trunk, branches and tendrils grow upwards at their own shape and pace. In faction the factual background is like a lattice on a wall. Instead of one's story being free to grow in any direction, it now has to weave its way upwards through the prescribed holes in the lattice.

This makes a story much harder to write, particularly if one's fiction is intermingled with social or political happenings in the past. We mentioned earlier the problems that time causes even in ordinary fiction. Now the story-line has to be twisted and convoluted so much to fit events and dates that there are moments when the author feels like throwing up the whole business and going into something simple like microprocessing or genetic engineering.

There's little doubt that, apart from the profit motive, this is the reason that some writers take the easy way out and change history to suit their meagre skills. For a writer with higher aspirations, I would suggest he leaves faction alone for his first two or three novels. Afterwards, when his plotting skills grow, I think he will find it a most rewarding, if exacting, form of writing.

16   Sequels and Series

Can we deal with books that evolve from an original work; in other words sequels or series. How would you define the difference?

My dictionary defines a sequel as a novel dealing with subsequent events in the lives of characters that have already appeared in a previous novel.

A series on the other hand is a number of books written about the same character or characters but with each story complete in itself and owing nothing in plot to the books before it, other than they have a similar flavour. The 633 SQUADRON series is an example of this. Many of the same characters are used in each book but every story stands on its own two feet.

Both types of work possess the same sales advantage. People begin to relate to the main characters. Sometimes, as on television, they even seem to believe they exist, and look forward to reading more about their adventures.

THE SERIES

Is it best to start from the premise that a novel is to be the first in a series?

I can't advise that. Far too many good ideas need an ending and if a writer were thinking all the time about subsequent books they would never be turned into successful novels. As I said earlier, a writer should always give his book the ending it deserves. In extreme cases this might need the death of a major character and while death could be called a natural ending, it hardly permits a follow-up.

On the other hand there are ideas or charismatic characters that do lend themselves to series or sequels, and if a writer has enough confidence while developing his plot to believe a subsequent book might be called for, then there is no doubt that the problems of continuity will be lessened in subsequent books if he structures his synopsis accordingly.

Certainly publishers are usually pleased to embark on a series or a sequel if the first novel does well. The effect is like a rolling snowball: each subsequent book making the subject more popular. In general, although by no means entirely, it is families and their business activities that provide the material for sequels, and charismatic characters like James Bond who are suited for a series.

You didn't, obviously, write 633 SQUADRON with a series in mind, since nearly all the major characters were killed off or lost as prisoners of war. Is that why seventeen years passed before you wrote the follow-up?

It was never my intention to write more than one book about the RAF. They say every novice writer needs to get one book out of his system and as I'd served over six years in the wartime RAF, 633 SQUADRON was mine, although it wasn't my first novel. I meant it as a small tribute to my friends, some of whom had been killed, and that was it. I never saw myself as a war novelist, nor do I today. I think of the 633 novels as anti-war books, and believe they are.

Then why did you eventually write the series?

There were a number of reasons but one was public pressure. Over the years 633 SQUADRON became what the publishers call a cult novel and I received hundreds of letters asking for a second book.

As you had killed off your characters in the first novel, how did you get round that problem when you eventually wrote the second novel?

I touched on that earlier. In the first novel I had a number of men wounded and hospitalised. I used them to form the backbone of the new squadron and made up its establishment by bringing in new crews.

No matter how long delayed, your decision to write these novels seems in contrast to your earlier warning about novelists not getting too involved in a series of similar books. How do you explain that?

I accept your point. I've already mentioned public pressure but apart from that I was extremely short of money at the time. This came about because a publisher's lack of foresight and a printers' strike had effectively killed a book I'd worked on for three years. As this was a financial crisis for me, I had little option but to accept a commission to write a series. I wrote three thrillers for the same reason. Sadly, the beliefs and aspirations of writers and their needs don't always go hand in hand.

However, before I accepted the publisher's offer, I had the thought that if I did a series of such books, they might serve to give a picture in the round of what life was like on an RAF operational squadron during World War Two before memories lost their clarity and crews were no longer alive.

As I said, I needed money at the time and the six books did well for me. At the same time, I can't deny some nostalgic pleasure in writing them. Any novelist who witnessed the high drama on wartime airfields would want to record it, just as he would want to pay tribute to the courage and sacrifices that he witnessed. My six RAF novels gave me the scope to do this, so it was no hardship to write them.

THE SEQUEL

Sequels present different problems to a series, of course. What is the best approach to them?

To be quite honest, most of their problems can be solved by commonsense. As we've just said, if a writer determines from the outset to write two or more books on an idea or theme, he is advised to develop a story-line in his first book that lends itself to sequels. Family dynasties are ideal for this purpose as the writer can progress from one generation to another. Women seem to specialise in this kind of fiction and the market is full of such books, usually with two rich families in conflict throughout the years.

Your own Yorkshire family trilogy would come into this category, wouldn't it?

To some extent, I suppose it would, although I like to think it is about real people and their problems. I find such people are much more interesting than melodramas about the rich and the powerful. On the other hand, no one's life, no matter how traumatic or appealing, is a novel in itself. Some embellishment is always necessary but it should never go over the top. It should always stay in balance with the incidents around it. This is, again, a matter of taste in writing.

Doesn't a sequel have a built-in problem in letting the reader know what happened in the earlier books? How do you overcome it without long explanatory narrative passages?

It is a problem because anyone who has read the first book will quickly become irritated by reading things he already knows. So the information must never be given in one solid chunk of narrative or dialogue. It should be fed into the story in bits and pieces so that this same reader is hardly aware he is receiving it.

This is best done by slotting the information in wherever it fits naturally. For example, if one is writing a sequel to an original novel set during a revolution, a talk on the radio about the revolution can be a pretext for sliding in memories of one of the main characters. The roar of a plane overheard might trigger off memories. Or the main character might meet an old revolutionary comrade, when relevant information can be fed into their conversation. And our old favourite, the dream, can also be used but only once or twice.

Whenever possible this information should be introduced in a way that advances the story-line as, for example, when the hero remembers some past incident that helps him overcome a present problem. This is an ideal method because it kills two birds with one stone but one is lucky if the chance comes more than once or twice.

It will be realised, of course, that these are much the same methods as one uses in flashbacks, only they are now used from one novel to another instead of within the contents of a single book.

Do you agree that a series avoids this problem of feeding in information, which is such a minefield for the sequel writer?

Yes, because with a different story-line for each novel, there is little or no call for flashbacks. The only need is to remind the reader about the hero or heroine's qualifications and even that need disappears when the characters become well known.

THE CHOICE

An important *don't* here is not to use detective or mystery plots if one wants to write a *sequel*. The reader would obviously feel cheated if the story wasn't solved at the end of the book. This type of plot is useless for sequels but ideal for a series, as the Agatha Christie stories prove.

To recap, a writer should never spoil a good idea by trying to manipulate its story-line to allow for a sequel or serial. That could cause his book to fall between two stools. If, however, he feels that his original idea might lend itself to a further book, then some attention to his synopsis might pay dividends later. If, on the other hand, the thought only comes to him while he is writing the book, he should take one vital precaution. Keep his main character or characters alive!

17 Revision

You've got the entire story down in writing but, as any first-class novelist knows, it's not yet a finished book. Do you launch straight into revision or do you pause for thought first?

I always think of my first manuscript as a piece of sculpture. In one sense it is finished in that the hunk of stone or marble has been cut down to size and does resemble to some extent the horse, elephant, or whatever creature I intended to create. It still needs many more touches, however. A little stone has to be chiselled off the neck, some from the belly, more off the buttocks - I chisel here and I chisel there and keep standing back to view the perspective until at last I feel it is as near a facsimile of the animal as I can achieve. I won't be completely satisfied - no artist ever is unless he is over the hill - but I'll feel it is the best I can do without going mad.

It is exactly the same procedure with a novel. Unless you're a genius - and what are they but people who take infinite care over their work - you edit and edit until you believe you can do no more.

This, however, is seldom true, and after this revision, my advice to the writer is to put the manuscript aside for a couple of weeks to distance himself from it. Then to read it right through as a reader would. Astonishingly, he will still find faults. There'll be poor sentences, words he has used too many times, sometimes even an entire chapter that he feels either ought to be condensed or put in a different place. He mustn't be a coward - although God knows it takes courage to take apart something on which he's worked so long. He must grit his teeth and make the changes.

The total time of editing might take months. Some authors take as long over it as in writing the novel itself. In some ways it is like polishing a stone. If the editing is done well the fire within it will become more brilliant the more it is worked on. I know there are some writers who say you can polish a manuscript so much that you destroy its fire but personally I've never found a novel of mine that hasn't improved with each polish. The only things that stop me are weariness and the cost in time. If one goes on too long, one can get to the point of hating the work - yes, I've felt that more than once - so a writer must use his discretion and know when to stop.

THE ULTIMATE AIM

Students often say: "I kept revising as I went along, so the book should be all right." But will it? What is revision intended to achieve?

The purpose of revision is to prune out all unnecessary verbiage, which includes irrelevant incidents and dialogue. In other words, its aim is brevity and clarity, which will result in a novel leaving a powerful impression on a reader's mind.

As I said earlier, this will be best achieved when the novel is completed in first draft, because this is the time when elements can be compared against one another and the correct proportion be judged. It also enables a writer to see his 'purple passages' in their true perspective. When they are being written, the writer is often emotionally involved and so has either over-written them or made them too long. Now that he has distanced himself from them, he is better able to judge whether they are valid or whether they need abbreviating.

At this point facts should also be checked, both to see they are correct and also to ensure they are necessary to the story-line and not present merely because the writer has felt they are of interest in themselves. At the risk of repetition, it should be stressed again that a modern novel should contain nothing extraneous to its aim and purpose.

Nevertheless, when carrying out this checking and pruning, the writer must bear one essential fact in mind. He must never weaken the vitality of his novel, because vitality is the one element that allows faults to be overlooked or even forgiven.

With the advent of modern technology, the word processor must have speeded up the business of editing. Has this proved a help to you, and would you recommend a PCW to all writers?

A word processor is an absolute godsend to anyone editing a script. If a novel has been written on one, all the laborious process of editing is made infinitely easier by the word processor's ability to pop words into sentences, entire phrases into chapters, or completely change the order of text. The saving that entails in laborious re-typing is quite astonishing. In the past I would spend months editing a book. My last book took me eleven days when I used a PCW.

BEST FRIEND: BEST ADVICE?

A writer feels an eager pride when his first novel is completed. But is a close friend or a family member the most suitable person to ask for an opinion?

In general I would say no. The closer the relationship, the less able a person feels to be critical (unless, of course, there are family bickerings, in which case a writer might get more criticism than he deserves!). Apart from the diffidences caused by the relationship, there is also the likelihood that the person is unqualified to act as an assessor.

It is far better to ask an objective critic to read one's novel, if the need is felt for an opinion. But, as stated earlier, a writer's best critic should be himself, and he should not spare himself in developing this faculty.

PUBLISHER'S ADVICE

Let us look forward one step. If a publisher should express interest in a manuscript but suggest certain revisions, how far should an author agree?

So much depends on the editor. A good one acts like the objective critic we've just talked about, and a sensible writer should at least pay attention to his suggestions. If the writer is a beginner, the odds are a hundred to one that the editor is right and his suggestions will improve the novel. Moreover, the editor is unlikely to accept the work if his advice is ignored.

On the other hand, there is a danger that the editor's advice might be commercially orientated, and an artistic novel can be ruined if popular elements are introduced. In such circumstances, only the author himself can decide what to do.

However, for the average genre novel, the editor is far more likely to be right than wrong, and the author would be wise to follow his advice unless the changes are so drastic that the book has to be virtually re-written. Then the author has to decide whether he can face re-jigging all the elements again. If he finds the task too daunting, then he could try another publisher with the book while he commences work on a new one.

Wasn't this kind of massive re-write suggested to you by the publishers of OF MASKS AND MINDS?

Yes, although the publisher wasn't criticising the story in itself but the way I had interpreted and used the medical facts on which it was based. This came about because he had sent the manuscript to a consultant psychiatrist who, no doubt because I was a medical layman, had damned every scene where the medical elements were involved. After sending me this consultant's report, the publisher announced that if I re-worked the novel to meet these criticisms, he would then accept and publish it.

This put me in an impossible situation because, had I met these demands, the entire premise on which the story was based would have disappeared. In other words, there would be no story.

Luck saved me. By an accident too lengthy to describe here, I met a psychiatrist who offered to read my manuscript over the weekend.

When I called at his surgery on the Monday, fully prepared to hear the worst, I was amazed to be told he had found nothing wrong with my interpretation and usage of the psychiatric details. Indeed, he went even further and said he had found some of the medical ideas I'd put into the story both novel and interesting.

Puzzled how two psychiatrists could differ so much in their professional opinions, but not such a fool as to labour the point, I asked if I might have a letter giving this very different opinion of my novel. This letter was sent to my publisher, who asked to see the manuscript again. Whether he called for a third opinion, I do not know, but in any case the novel was published some months later without a word being changed.

If there is a lesson in this story, it is perhaps that editors are as human as the rest of us, and a writer should bear this in mind while at the same time being open to fair and reasonable criticism.

PRESENTATION

So we have written the novel under the conditions specified earlier and have edited it to the best of our time and ability. What is the next move?

For a beginner, or near beginner, I would make a suggestion at this point. Before you go to the expense of having your novel typed or spend the long hours typing a final, presentable copy yourself, let an experienced novel assessor read it for you. We all make mistakes, technical and otherwise, and some might affect whole chapters of our book. And for a reason perhaps only psychologists can explain, we sometimes can't pick out these mistakes ourselves even though we read our story time and again.

An objective and experienced assessor will find these mistakes much more easily. He will also point out spelling mistakes and the wrong usage of words. It might cost a few pounds but you will also get advice on the construction of your story and the difference might well be the difference between acceptance and refusal.

At one time all publishers employed copy-editors to read a book, even after they'd accepted it, and it was a great comfort for writers, even experienced ones, to know their work was being thoroughly and competently vetted before it went out to the public. Today, with a few praiseworthy exceptions, the standard of in-house copy-editing is such that even professional writers sometimes pay privately for their scripts to be vetted, if only for their peace of mind. I have already mentioned how readers love to pick out faults and write in about them!

This type of editing, of course, applies to novels that appear in manuscript form. But today some publishers are asking their authors to submit PCW discs instead of manuscripts, and this trend is likely to grow. This calls for even greater care by the author because published copies will be printed straight from the discs and any mistake is less likely to be picked up by the printer. So copy-editing becomes even more necessary when PCWs are used.

You, as a copy-editor yourself, will know there are plenty of these freelance copy-editors about but good ones are relatively thin on the ground. So a beginner should ask advice before he submits his manuscript to them.

I have to agree with you, haven't I? Assuming this copy-editing has been done or a writer has decided the novel can stand as it is, what are the basic rules that govern its manuscript presentation?

Good quality A4 paper should be used, and the writer should have an original and two carbon copies typed or printed. One of these copies he should always keep, both for reference and insurance against the manuscript's loss. For work prepared on a word processor, at least one back-up copy of the disc/discs should be made as a safeguard against accident or damage to the master copy.

Publishers ask that you type in double line spacing, allowing at least $1\frac{1}{2}''$ of margin all round the text.

The first sheet should be the title page. The title should be set in capitals in the centre of the page and unless a PCW has been used (which will give the exact number of words), the approximate length of the novel should be given beneath it. To gain this approximation, the words on five pages that have an average mixture of text and dialogue should be counted and the result divided by five. The result should then by multiplied by the total number of pages in the novel, which will give a fair indication of its length.

The author's name should be set at the foot of this page with a circled Ⓒ before it and the current year after it. This is to establish the book belongs to the author and he owns the copyright.

The second page, which will be one of the flyleaves of the printed book, should contain a courtesy acknowledgement of any books that have been used for reference purposes, giving their titles, their publishers, and their authors. This page can also contain any dedication that the author wishes to make to a helper, friend, or relative.

The third page should contain the titles of any other books the author might have published. The fourth page should be the first page of his novel. It should be headed Chapter 1, after which the final typing can begin, with the typist remembering to indent a few spaces for each new paragraph, not forgetting the ample margins and reasonable spacing between each line. This makes for easy reading and also allows copy-editors and printers to make comments or corrections.

Do not paginate the book chapter by chapter. Start with page one and paginate right through to the end. This is because it is a good practice to send an agent or publisher the manuscript in loose pages - he can then take parts of it home from the office at nights to read without having to carry its full weight. So it is better not to bind the manuscript but to enclose it in a strong cardboard folder or in a box.

It's all ready. How does our hopeful author choose a publisher to send it to? Would you recommend a preliminary letter and synopsis first, or send the entire manuscript and a covering letter?

At this point, of course, a writer could send his book to an agent instead of a publisher. However, as I would like to discuss this choice in more detail later, let us assume for the moment he has decided on a publisher. If he hasn't a name in mind, he should look through the various year books to find the one most likely to take his type of novel. If he has any doubts about this, he can always give the publisher a quick phone call to ensure his choice is correct.

Assuming it is, then in my opinion he should write a short but competent letter subtly emphasising his novel's merits. He should enclose this letter with his manuscript (not forgetting to enclose either sufficient stamps or an equivalent postal order/cheque for its return), wrap up the entire package, and post it off.

Lastly, on his way home, it would be no bad thing if he were to say a little prayer or cross his fingers, for the football pools and the writing profession have much in common!

ILLUSTRATION 13: The all-important letter

Publishers and/or agents are busy people and a great many manuscripts land daily on their desks. A letter, enclosed with your manuscript, should point out the book's strong points, and emphasise the theme it addresses.

Take care, firstly, to find out the name of the company's editor dealing with fiction submissions.

Mr Jonathon Thistleberry,
Editorial Director (Fiction),
McWilliams Publishing Ltd,
Gardenfields
LONDON EC1 9RQ

Dear Mr Thistleberry,

re: Novel, OF MASKS AND MINDS by _____

I am enclosing a copy of my recently completed first novel,
which has the title Of Masks and Minds.

Set in a large middle-class family home in Devon, it deals
with the problems encountered when the major character, a
young married woman, finds the husband she loves very
deeply, seriously ill and deteriorating rapidly.

A psychological novel, it asks the question 'What is the
price of a man's sanity?' - one of the most serious problems
facing today's medical men and, inevitably, wives and
families.

As the husband, a composer, steadily loses his reason, his
wife is faced with a terrible dilemma: she can agree to a
pre-frontal leucotomy operation which will restore his
senses, but which would, in all probability, destroy his
creative talent. Or leave the illness to destroy him,
because although his mind is going, he is writing better
music as it does. Beethoven was a neurotic, wrestling with
God: James Allister has only the darkness of mind to wrestle
with.

Hers is a fearful situation, terrifying in its loneliness.
Tortured by her husband's black moods, harassed by relatives
who can see no reason against the operation, she grasps at a
third alternative - in uncovering the guilt that is driving
him insane - only to find her dilemma deeper than ever.

I enclose the manuscript and postage for its return should
you find it unsuitable for McWilliams' list.

Part Two

18 Agent or Publisher for a First Novel?

A question I am always asked after I have assessed a novel, is where the writer should send it, to an agent or a publisher. What do you think?

I have no hesitation whatever in answering this question. It is to a publisher. My reason is as follows:

Unless a writer's work is outstanding, he will be extremely unlikely to find a *good* agent who will take him on in his early days. Good agents take on only as many writers as they can adequately handle, which means they always have a queue of skilled writers desiring their services. Then why should they take on a beginner when they can have proven writers who will bring them in an immediate income?

The answer is they won't and they don't. A beginner will get a good agent when he has proved himself and that is the best he can hope for.

To be truthful, these days he might even find it difficult to get a bad agent because with so many people wanting to write, this type of agent usually takes on more clients than he can adequately handle. He gets round this by seeking only the plum sales, like volume rights and perhaps a major magazine serial rights, and ignoring all the smaller outlets. He does this because sales in these lesser markets would bring in only small commissions. Yet these sales mean so much to struggling writers.

Don't, therefore, envy writers who have such agents. Pity them instead because they are living in a fool's paradise. Having slaved for a year or more on a book, they are now dreaming dreams about their manuscripts being conscientiously sent from one important publisher to the next. The truth is they will be sent out two or three times with a sterile printed slip stuck into their flyleaves and that will be the sum total of their travels. Postage costs are high and two or three rejections are usually enough for this kind of agent. While the author dreams his dreams, his masterpiece is lying in a drawer gathering dust.

Does this mean that you haven't a high regard for agents in general?

No, I wouldn't say that. With one exception, I've been fairly treated by agents. But this is because, after an experience I had in the Fifties, I choose them carefully. I had managed to get my first novel accepted by one of London's so-called top agencies (which, come to think of it, was something of a miracle in itself), and believing I would now be well looked after, I dreamed my dreams for the next ten months while unpaid bills piled up around me.

Of course, I didn't waste these months: no writer should do that. I spent them working on my second novel but even so, visions kept entering my mind of important publishers all over London reading my first masterpiece.

It was only after I wrote the agent half a dozen letters that went unanswered that doubts began creeping into my mind. So I borrowed the train fare to London, went to the agency, and asked about my novel. The first girl I addressed looked blank and moved away to whisper to a second one. She looked equally blank and the two of them withdrew to the back of the office where they began rummaging around in a large cabinet. Finally they started dragging out piles of manuscripts until after fifteen minutes or so the first girl gave a low cry of triumph and showed one to her colleague. Glancing furtively round, she blew dust off its folder before she came forward and handed it to me.

I discovered the novel had been sent to three publishing houses and that was all. Fortunately I had the sense to grab it and run, otherwise it is unlikely I would ever have become a full time novelist.

At that point you were presumably disinclined to seek out another agent. Did you decide to go it alone?

I went home, bought myself a Writers' and Artists' Year Book, looked to see which publishers were likely to be interested in the subject of the novel, and then sent it out.

It came back and I sent it out! It came back and I sent it out! No, the waiting wasn't as bad as before. It wasn't a quarter as bad. The reason was that I was now controlling its destiny. I knew that it was going to this and that publisher and so every day there was the chance it might be taken. I began to look forward to my mail again, even if it did only bring rejection slips. At least they were evidence the book was being seen and considered.

Perhaps the feeling resembles that of a woman who has just had a baby. She's not happy to leave it in someone else's hands. She wants to be the one who feeds it, washes it, and even changes its nappies. Not to be sitting alone wondering if it is being cared for, or neglected by, a stranger.

The move certainly paid off for me. Eighteen months and thirteen publishers later the novel was accepted. In turn the publisher sold serial rights and the film rights. If I had left the manuscript with that agency it would still be an unpublished book.

I'm not for one moment suggesting all agencies are as inefficient as this. Good ones will let a writer know when they have given up submitting his manuscript and will return it to him. Bad agents, however, will waste time quite disgracefully in their handling of an author's work, knowing that if they leave it in a drawer for months, a novice author will assume they have been conscientiously sending it out all that time.

This underlines the problems of writers. So much of the profession is in the hands of uncreative people who know little, and care even less, about the effort and time that goes into the writing of a dramatic work.

This ignorance and off-handedness does not only apply to agents. There are plenty of publishers who quite shamelessly will keep a manuscript months or even years without saying yea or nay.

CHOOSING A PUBLISHER

So the newly completed novel is going straight to a publisher. The author has a list of publishing house names, but where does he start?

He must first study the market to see which publishing houses are likely to be interested in his novel. It will waste time and money to send a racy crime story to a publisher specialising in 'straight' or 'academic' fiction. Preferences are given in the year books, but if a writer still has doubts, he can always phone publishing houses to check if the subject of his novel is suitable for them.

Once he has made a list of the possible markets, he has to decide whether he wants a large or a small publishing house. The larger ones, with a highly profitable list of best selling authors are, on the whole, more likely to take the risk of losing money on a first novel, although their acceptance will depend on whether they believe the author has enough promise to make them money with future books. A further advantage is that they can *afford* to give the beginner a larger advance and provide better marketing facilities than the smaller houses.

I stress *afford,* however, because not all large publishing houses pay more than smaller ones. Some, indeed, pay less. Moreover, a beginner often needs guidance and counselling after his first novel is accepted, and he is much more likely to get such personal attention from a smaller house than from a large one, where he is often made to feel the very small fish that he is.

So the wise beginner bears these points in mind before making his choice and posting off his novel.

In your opinion how long should a writer wait for a decision?

From a reputable publisher, two months at the very most because after that time a work is unlikely to be still under consideration.

But new writers are so afraid that an enquiry might bring about a rejection.

I know that, but the truth is publishers are in the business of obtaining good material and they aren't going to turn a novel down simply because its author has the good sense to ask what is happening to it. If they are considering it, all an enquiry will do is bring a letter to that effect. If on the other hand a query brings the book back, it simply means it has jolted someone into sending the book back earlier than they would otherwise have done. It certainly has not caused the rejection in itself. At least having the novel returned saves the author precious time to make submissions elsewhere.

I am often asked if publishers give priority to novels sent in by agents. What do you think?

If the agent is a good one, it is probably true because it means the novel has already had one reading and so has passed its first test. But this brings the novice back to the problem of how he gets this good agent. A novel sent in by a bad agent - and publishers, not being fools, know who they are - will gain no more attention than if it came directly from the author.

Remember that publishers have their own reading staff whose job is to look at every manuscript that is sent in. Unless the book is good, they don't usually read the entire work but then they don't need to. Wasn't it Dr Johnson who said it isn't necessary to eat the whole ox to find out if the beef is tough? An experienced reader can tell from the first few pages whether a work has quality or not. If it has, it will then be read just as thoroughly as if the best agent in Britain had sent it in. So, agent or no agent, a novel will still receive attention.

I take it that you still recommend the Writers' and Artists' Year Book and/or The Writers' Handbook as sources of information on publishers and agents?

Yes, I've always used them, although with postage so expensive, it isn't a bad idea, as I suggested earlier, to give a publisher a ring before a writer posts his book to him to make certain it fits his requirements. As copies of his novel are valuable, he should always enclose return postage with the manuscript.

GENERAL TIPS ON MARKETING WORK

What tips would you give a beginner when sending out his work?

I'm a firm believer in sending with my submission the kind of letter

I mentioned earlier, one that sets out my book's most important elements. Publishers (and agents too, for that matter) are busy people and they will often miss things if they aren't pointed out. Nor should one be over modest in this letter. In the world today a man is often judged by his belief in himself, so let that belief come through.

To emphasise this point, an agent I was using had a book of mine turned down by a well-known publisher who until then had liked my work. Unable to understand this refusal, I suggested that my agent send it again with a letter stressing the points that I felt would interest the editor. Somewhat expectedly, my agent felt unable to do this, so I suggested I did it myself. Hesitantly he agreed, and I posted the manuscript back with a letter that I spent a full day honing and polishing. The outcome? The book was taken without a murmur.

Undoubtedly the letter was the secret. I had not written a long one - that can put an editor off - but I had written a good one emphasising certain points in the novel that I knew the editor would like. The fact that these had been brought to his attention had given the book its second chance.

DEALING WITH REJECTION

Rejection so often depresses beginners. Many think it means their book is a failure. Yet your first novel was rejected sixteen times before acceptance. How do you see rejection slips?

A publisher can reject a novel for reasons that have no bearing on its quality. He might be the wrong publisher for that type of book. He might have recently published a book on a similar subject and does not want to follow it with a second one so soon. His reader might have made a false judgement. He, the editor, might have had indigestion that morning or had a quarrel with his wife.

A writer should not even think about giving up until he has tried at least a dozen publishers. As you say, my first novel went to sixteen before it was taken. At the same time, take notice of any comments the editors might give you along with their rejection slips, and if you feel they are valid, make the necessary amendments.

WHEN THE NOVEL IS ACCEPTED

Let's be optimistic and assume a beginner has his novel accepted. What should he do next?

In my opinion this is the proper time to take on an agent. Although a writer has found a buyer for his 'goods', he must remember that in doing so he has entered the bold, bad world of business, which in effect means he must now doff his writer's hat and put on his tin helmet. That is why I have used the word 'goods' for a novel, because sadly that is what it has now become.

The urbane publisher who might wine and dine our writer is very skilled at manipulating novices and obtaining their novels as cheaply as possible. As he is doing this for his firm and his shareholders, one can't condemn him too harshly for it, but at the same time the beginner must be on his guard. The usual method, done with the utmost charm, is to make a good novel appear a very average one. Indeed, after a few glasses of wine, the poor bemused author is in danger of feeling heartfelt gratitude towards a publisher who is prepared to pay him any money at all for such an amateurish effort!

The result can be seen all the way throughout the writing profession. One sees poor authors on every street corner but one seldom, if ever, sees a poor publisher. This is why once a writer has received a favourable response from one he should scuttle off to find himself a good agent. This should be done *before* he accepts the publisher's offer: the timing is most important.

But didn't you say a beginner has little chance of obtaining a good agent?

That was *before* he had a publisher interested in his work. With a letter in his pocket expressing that interest, there should be no difficulty now. That letter is proof the writer has talent and, perhaps more importantly, it means the agent is going to make immediate money out of him. I've never met an agent yet, good or bad, who can resist that inducement.

All the same, writers will want to know why they need an agent after they've done all the donkey work themselves in selling their novel.

I have partly answered that question by showing that the best person to handle a publisher is another business man. A good agent will not only know the publisher and how much he can pay, he will also be able to estimate the value of the writer's novel. He can sit at a table with the publisher and say: "Come off it, John! This is a good novel and worth twice as much as you're offering." The author, unless he is unusually confident and tough-skinned, can't say this of his own work and so will get a smaller offer. The agent might not get the double figure that he asks for but he is likely to get enough both to cover his commission and to leave the writer better off than he would have been without him.

The benefit of this procedure will already have been realised. Not only has the writer now got a publisher who will give serious consideration to his second book but he has also got a good agent who, because the writer has earned him money, should take good care of him in the future.

AFTER PUBLICATION

Would you recommend the author of a newly published novel (or accepted for publication) to join a professional body? What are the advantages?

Most certainly. There are two I recommend. The Writers' Guild of Great Britain is a TUC affiliated trade union which offers help and guidance concerning agents and publishers and gives advice on all aspects of authorship. It also takes up complaints in areas such as breaches of contract and copyright infringements. It will vet literary contracts for a member and will also take up the cudgel for him if it appears he is being badly treated or exploited.

The Society of Authors is an independent professional body which offers the same help and protection. Both societies, which have an excellent relationship with one another, are in the forefront of campaigns on behalf of authors.

In my opinion, the moment a writer gets a novel accepted or published, he should approach one or the other for membership. Alone and defenceless, writers are easy prey. No worker in the nation needs more support than we do and the Societies give us that support.

There is yet another reason why these societies deserve our membership. It was they who helped us win Public Lending Rights. They are also ceaseless in their efforts to improve our lot in all the media that use our work. Join one or the other and a writer will gain the confidence he needs to handle publishers and agents alike. After all, if he feels diffident about arguing a point with one of them, it's a lovely cop out to say: "For myself I'd agree but you see I can't because the Guild or Society wouldn't approve of it." We authors have to be cunning as well as brave!

19 Agents

FINDING A GOOD ONE

How are good agents found? This is a question my students are always asking me. Have you any suggestions to offer?

This is not an easy matter. The very best ones seldom advertise because they already have enough clients. Some of the good ones do not even bother to have their names in the writers' year books.

A would-be author's best move is to join a writers' circle and/or attend one of the many writers' conferences that are held all over the country. With any luck he will encounter published authors who, over a glass of wine, will recommend this or that agent. One word of warning here, however. Only seek advice from experienced writers who know a good agent when they see one. A recommendation from a novice might be worse than no recommendation at all.

If this method fails, or is not possible, then a writer will have to rely on the year books which on the whole list only agents of repute. But remember that some agents specialise in certain areas of the market, so the author should make certain the one he approaches handles the type of fiction he writes.

How do you define a good agent?

I suggest asking the following questions:

1 Is he approachable or does he believe he is God? If he acts like the Divinity (and some do), then don't become one of his submissive little angels. Writers are vulnerable people in a precarious profession and although they shouldn't become a nuisance to their agents, they do occasionally need someone to talk over their problems with. If the agent has not got the time, understanding, or humanity to allow this, he is not in my opinion a suitable manager for a novice writer.

2 Will he read one's work himself? Some agents don't do this. They give out books to readers who assess the books for them. I don't object to this procedure if the readers are expert assessors because this leaves the agent more time to market good books instead of wasting his time on ones that have no hope of publication. But once a reader has recommended a book, I maintain an agent should always read it himself before sending it to a publisher. It is the only way he can find enthusiasm for a work and it is so often enthusiasm that sways a publisher.

3   Will he, at mutually agreed periods, send the writer a list of the markets he has tried with his novel? Nearly all agents hate to do this but I cannot see why they should. An author might have a year's work and money invested in a book. Surely this gives him a right to know what is happening to it? A writer should be a good business man and make certain his product is being efficiently marketed.

4   Does the agent ask for a preliminary reading fee? It is true that more and more agents are doing this these days but it isn't a practice that I like because the agents who used to do it in the past were usually shysters and how does a novice tell the difference between one and the other if it becomes common practice? In my opinion the only money an agent should get from a writer is a percentage of anything he sells. This should be 10 per cent, although because of higher all-round costs, many agents are asking for 15 per cent these days. For foreign sales he will ask for 20 per cent. This is reasonable because most agents sell foreign language rights through their counterparts abroad and these agents have to be paid their 10 per cent for making the sale.

5   If the writer is a novice, will the agent give advice on his work? Some writers like this, others hate it. If a writer belongs to the former group, he will want the question answering. If the agent's reply is yes, it shows two things. He reads one's work himself and he sees promise in it. But a writer should remember one thing if he gets advice from agents or publishers. Unless they belong to the highest professional bracket, their advice will be commercially orientated.

There is nothing wrong with this kind of advice if a writer is writing solely for money. Nor need he be ashamed if he is. As I said earlier, nearly everyone else in society works for money, so why not authors? But if a writer has more literary inclinations and he feels that his work might lose integrity by following their advice, then he has every right to decline to take it, but politely, because they are only trying to help him.

6   There is a final point to remember when considering an agent. He earns his living from selling a writer's work. This raises an ethical point that in my experience few authors consider but which I believe is an important yardstick in assessing the integrity of an agent. There are not that many really good publishers. There are, on the other hand, many authors, good, bad, and indifferent. What, then, does an agent do when there is a serious clash of interests between one of his authors and one of the leading publishers and there is little to choose between their contentions?

Provided the writer's case is a fair one, there should be no hesitation in a good agent's mind. It is the writer who is paying him and therefore it is the writer for whom he should fight. And in all fairness this is what good agents do.

But consider how a bad agent's mind might work. If he takes the writer's side and it costs the publisher money, might that not incline the publisher to take fewer of his other submissions? Once that thought strikes him, it becomes easy to justify his siding with the publisher. He might even convince himself that to do otherwise would not be fair to his other authors who use or need that same publisher.

I accept this is not a frequent occurrence but as we are now in the business world, commonsense tells us it must sometimes happen. As I say, the good agent will always fight for his authors and the good publishers will expect nothing less. Indeed they will like and respect him for it. The danger only arises when a poverty of soul exists in both the agent and the publisher. Then an author could find he is being sold short. If an author suspects his agent is not fully behind him in his dealings with publishers, he should leave him at once.

APPROACHING THE AGENT

What is the best initial approach to an agent - a telephone call, a letter, the finished manuscript?

For a writer seeking to obtain an agent before trying a publisher with his work, I believe his best approach is to write the agent, enclose a sample of his previous work, and the first chapter or so of the novel he would like the agent to negotiate. This allows the agent to assess his talent and the likelihood of publication.

As no matter how great his expenses, an agent only receives between 10 per cent and 15 per cent of any proceeds from a writer's work, the better one needs to know if a new novelist is capable of earning enough in the future to make him a commercially viable proposition for his company. This estimated figure will vary from agent to agent but a top class agency might expect a writer to earn at least £10,000 per annum.

But, as I have said, a writer should not try to get an agent until a publisher shows interest in his novel. The agent then knows the novel is publishable and so is much more likely to take on the author.

If he does, the terms and conditions of both parties should be mutually discussed to ensure no misunderstandings occur. If the writer doesn't find the agent's terms satisfactory, he should, of course, look elsewhere.

But assuming the terms are satisfactory, the agent can then begin negotiations with the publisher. The likelihood now is that he will gain a better contract than the writer alone would have obtained. A good agent will also counsel the novice writer and save him a good deal of anxiety.

In turn the writer should respect his agent and not pester him with too many phone calls which, in any case, shouldn't be necessary if the agent lets the writer know what is happening to his work.

At the same time a writer should not be in awe of agents and publishers as so many writers seem to be. One should not be afraid to establish the terms of one's relationship. Remember what Samuel Johnson said: "The chief glory of every people arises from its authors." Keep that in mind and remember always that agents, publishers, editors, bookbinders, Uncle Tom Cobley and all, could not survive without us. We are the tree from which all these branches flourish, so a writer should stand up for his rights without showing arrogance, inconsideration, or discourtesy.

LEAVING AN AGENT

Another question I am often asked is can an author give notice to an agent without complications or ill feeling? Some beginners imagine they will be tied for ever to an agent once he has accepted their work.

A writer is not tied in any way to an agent unless he has signed a contract with him. Few agents ask for this but if they do, I would advise a writer not to sign one in case of dissatisfaction later. At the same time, a writer should play fair with his agent by not moving his books about just for the sake of it. Loyalty should exist on both sides and a relationship that possesses it has no need for written contracts.

What happens if a partnership does break up?

Each side should give the other fair and adequate notice in writing. The author should also remember that the agent has a right to continue collecting commission on books that he has sold even if those sales continue long into the future.

THE AGENT AND THE CONTRACT

The reputable agent should be the author's insurance against ill-drafted contracts which sell him short. Should the author rely on this?

The author should rely on nobody but himself in all his business dealing. No matter how good an agent is, no matter if he tells the writer the contract has been carefully checked and he can sign on the dotted line with impunity, the writer should never dream of doing any such thing until he has read every word himself. Carelessness among office staff is endemic these days and the writer is the loser if errors have been made and gone uncorrected. This advice comes from the heart because of the money I have lost and the problems I've been caused by faulty contracts. Now I not only read every word: I also check every comma and full stop.

20   Publishers and Responsibilities

What in your view distinguishes a good publisher?

I'll list the qualities I believe he should have:

1 He should understand and respect his authors.

2 He should give his authors fair and equitable contracts.

3 He should see the author receives the proofs of a book with plenty of time allowed for checking.

4 He should consult him about the book jacket.

5 He should give the author twelve free copies.

6 He should advertise the book prominently in the trade journals and, possibly, in one or two of the major newspapers.

7 He should ensure his representatives try to sell the book with enthusiasm. To do otherwise is to sell the author short.

8 He should pay promptly according to the terms of his contract.

9 He should let the author know in advance that he is letting the book go out of print.

PROOFS AND CORRECTIONS

I feel some of these points need explaining. Looking at proofs in more detail, what is the problem with the time-scale of proof copies of the novel and any necessary changes to the text?

Page proofs are the printer's first copy of the book - his first draft, if you like. It is the author's right to see these, and they are sent to him for two reasons: one, so that he can make any last minute changes to his book and two, to correct any mistakes he or the printer might have made. As every full stop and comma has to be checked against the copy-edited typescript from which the proofs have been set, it is a tedious task. To identify changes or corrections, the author uses standard proof symbols and the publisher asks him to identify which mistakes are his own and which are the printers by the use of different colour markings. Great care must be taken, because if the author misses anything it is more than likely the mistake will appear in the published book.

As for the author's changes to his text, he must take care to keep these down to the minimum because there is usually a clause in the contract that commits him to pay for more than 10 per cent of *his own* text alterations. He can, however, reduce any such charges by inserting words of the same length as those he has cut out. This will avoid the complications of re-jigging pages, an exercise that is both time consuming and expensive.

My point concerning time-scale was that proofs sometimes reach the author with a note saying they must be returned in a week or so or the book won't meet its publication deadline. This sloppy practice can mean an author missing his holidays, as has happened to me twice, and is unnecessary if the publisher is on top of his job.

Everyone involved in the process needs, therefore, to ensure that his part is done as quickly and responsibly as possible?

Yes. An author should fulfil his obligations by submitting a manuscript as free from grammatical and factual errors as possible. This will avoid substantial alterations at the proof stage. Equally, the book's editor should discuss the publication schedule with the author in advance, taking into account the business and social commitments of all concerned - not forgetting the growing number of national public holidays that close down firms for days, even weeks, at a time.

Such consultation allows everyone involved to keep as closely as possible to the schedule, and allows everyone a fair share of the time-scale. All too often the author is given the least consideration and is left working under unnecessary pressure to make up for the laxity of others.

Giving the author reasonable time to do his checking also prevents him from going boggle-eyed searching for printers' errors, which these days are scattered about like leaves in autumn. My diary tells me that in my first novel, published in 1954, there were forty-seven printer's errors. In a recent novel I counted over one thousand, two hundred! Such is modern progress.

THE BOOK JACKET

You suggest a publisher should consult authors over their book jackets. With Sales Managers wielding such power these days, do you think this is likely?

With jackets of naked women advertising books on anything from brothels to the Scriptures, I think it is eminently sensible if publishers want to win back the trust of the public. I'm fully aware that Sales Directors will scoff at me for even suggesting it, but it's my contention that publishers have the most to gain by at least asking for an author's suggestions. After all, who knows his book better than he? Book shops tell us that a good jacket can be a great aid to a book's sales. Then doesn't it equally follow that a bad one can have the reverse effect?

Let me give two cases in point. Not long ago I had a novel published about a young English married couple caught up in the First World War. Because of its subject, half the book was devoted to the young man's life in the British trenches and the other half to his wife's traumas back in England. I accept this did not make it an easy jacket to design but nevertheless a little ingenuity could easily have solved the problem.

Instead, when I received a courtesy copy of the novel, I found its jacket depicted a grizzled French soldier in a trench. A *French* soldier! When I rang up the publisher I was told the mistake was due to a production manager not knowing the difference between a French and a British soldier's uniform.

In spite of my frantic protests, I was told that nothing could be done to rectify the mistake because books had already gone out to the critics and distributors. In my opinion the poor sales that followed were a possible result of that tragic jacket because the few critics who forced themselves to read on past it gave the book excellent reviews. Eighteen months of meticulous work had been spoiled. At such times it is difficult to express the feelings of an author.

Another version on the same theme occurred with the sixth of my 633 SQUADRON novels, OPERATION TITAN. As mentioned earlier, the structure of this story was built around a target whose nature, for security reasons, could not be divulged until the last moment. With the plot demanding that the secret should be kept from the reader too, it was a difficult formula and meant a great deal of work for me, but eventually I was quite pleased with the result.

That is I was pleased until the American and English paperback versions came out. Need I say what they displayed? The very target itself, a bridge over a river, being bombed by aircraft! A lack of perception in some art directors can be quite breathtaking.

In contrast, the English hardcover publishers of these novels allowed me to have a say in the jackets. A friend and myself joined forces and designed one suitable for each novel in the series. The publisher accepted it and told me later that it had been extremely popular with booksellers and public alike and had aided the sale of the books.

None of this means I am suggesting authors should take over the role of jacket designers. One accepts that sales directors should know more about eye-catching designs than writers. But if art directors paid more attention to their authors' books, such disastrous mistakes could be avoided.

STALLING WITH PAYMENT

You indicate that publishers should pay their authors promptly. Are you suggesting that some don't?

In a recent survey carried out for the Society of Authors, it was found that only around 30 per cent of publishers kept to the terms of their contracts. The rest went weeks and months past their contractual time and a few even went years. Appropriately, the survey was called the Good, the Bad, and the Ugly.

These delays referred mostly to royalty payments. The publisher collates his sales figures every six months and then gives himself another three months to pay the author his royalties extracted from these sales. This means, once the system is in motion, the writer ought to get his royalties at half yearly intervals. In nearly 70 per cent of cases, the Guild found publishers were late on these payments.

OUT OF PRINT AND RIGHTS REVERTED

What was your point about the book going out of print?

When a publisher has decided a book has run its course, he 'pulps' or 'remainders' the overstock. That means he either turns the copies into paper pulp or sells them cheaply to the growing chain of remainder bookshops. If he doesn't tell the author of his intention, the author loses the chance of buying some, or all, of these cheap copies. Indeed he might find himself without any copies of his book at all.

One would think it only courtesy to warn an author of this intention but I've had more than one publisher deny it to me. Consequently a clause obliging the publisher to notify the author should always be in the contract. Another reason for prompt notification is that an author is entitled to claim the publication rights back once the book is no longer on the market. He does this by sending a letter to the publisher asking for the rights to be reverted to him nine months after the book has gone out of print. However, he clearly cannot do this if he isn't told the book is being withdrawn. In this way publishers sometimes hold the rights longer than they are entitled to.

This delay in notification can also cost the author money. If he gets the rights reverted, he can sell them again if his book should spring back into life. If he does not get them back, the original publisher can re-issue the book without paying him any advance at all.

PUBLISHERS GOOD AND BAD

From your experiences you would be justified in having a poor opinion of publishers, past and present. Is this so?

It would be both wrong and churlish of me to suggest there are no good publishers. Some existed in the past and a goodly number exist today, and I respect them. At the same time I believe publishers in general suffer the same handicap that all employers suffer when they have a non-unionised and acquiescent labour force - in this case too many writers who seem prepared to accept any conditions and any payment to see their work in print.

While such writers tend to deserve what they get, this is not good for publishers. With material coming to them so easily and cheaply, they are not called upon to sharpen their business faculties. The literary world is a little too warm and cosy.

Two other problems face publishing. One is its aesthetic image and the other its reputation of being one of the few remaining professions of the gentleman. These factors tend to saturate it with university arts graduates who, while educated to charm and impress, are not famous for the practical skills of management, organisation, and marketing. A few, indeed, give the impression they are too lofty for such sordid practices, although I admit this occurs more in hardcover houses than in softcover ones, which, because they are more mass market orientated, tend to employ a different kind of man.

In extreme cases this can lead to an author's interests being badly neglected. In case anyone thinks I am exaggerating, let me give an example of what happened to me. Back in the days when books had to be copyrighted in the United States or they went into the public domain, I lost an offer of film rights in a novel because my publisher had forgotten to ask his American agent to take the necessary action. As a consequence, with my book now in the open market for anyone to pick up without payment, my film offer was dropped like a hot potato. It was a catastrophe for a young novelist, yet the only apology I received from the publisher was: "These things happen from time to time."

These things should not happen. Nor would they if guilty publishers were to tighten up their working methods. But I fear that unless authors show more spirit and demand better treatment, the slipshod and occasionally cavalier ways of such publishing houses will continue.

21 Book Contracts

What are the terms of an average book contract?

Contracts vary considerably and unfortunately often omit clauses that are necessary for an author's interests. In Britain, the Writers' Guild of Great Britain and The Society of Authors recently drew up together a contract called a MINIMUM TERMS AGREEMENT. This is a kind of Bill of Rights Charter for authors that the two societies believe every author should urge his publisher to accept.

It should be noted that these are *minimum* terms. Even so, only a few publishers have so far agreed to the contract in its entirety. However, the two societies are working hard to draw all the laggards into this just and equitable net and all we authors should do our best to help them.

The Writers' Guild of Great Britain has kindly given permission to print this contract as it stands and so it appears on the following pages:

MINIMUM TERMS AGREEMENT

AN AGREEMENT made this   day of   198
between The Society of Authors and The Writers' Guild of Great
Britain of the one part and   (hereinafter
called "the Publishers") of the other part
WHEREBY IT IS AGREED AS FOLLOWS

A. Scope of Agreement

This Agreement contains the minimum terms and conditions to be
observed in all contracts ("the contract") between the Publishers
and all members of the Society of Authors and all members of the
Writers' Guild (any such members being called "the Author") in
respect of any original literary work published in hardcover volume
form but excluding the following categories:

1. Illustrated books defined as books which would not have been
   published save for the illustrations.

2. Technical books, manuals, reference works.

3. Textbooks written for the educational market (as distinct
   from general books of an academic or instructional nature).

4. Books involving three or more writers.

5. Plays and poetry.

B. Nature of Agreement

1. The terms and conditions of the contract shall be no less
   favourable to the Author nor in any way detract from or
   qualify the terms and conditions specified in Section C hereof.

2. This Agreement may be re-negotiated on either party giving to
   the other three months' written notice expiring at any time
   after the fifth anniversay hereof.

3. The contract shall contain the words "drafted in accordance
   with the Society of Authors/Writers' Guild Minimum Terms
   Agreement".

C. Terms of the Contract between the Author and the Publisher

1. Delivery & Acceptance of the Typescript

   (a) The Author shall deliver not later than the date specified
       in the contract one legible copy of the typescript of the
       work. The contract shall specify the fullest possible
       details of length, number and type of illustrations,
       index, etc. The Author shall deliver a script which, in
       style and content, is professionally competent and fit
       for publication.

   (b) The Publishers shall notify the Author of any changes
       required in the script within 30 days. Should the
       Publishers reject the script on the ground that it fails
       to meet the specifications in (a) above, they shall within
       30 days provide the Author with written notice of not less
       than 250 words in which the grounds for rejecting the
       script shall be set out in such a manner as to facilitate
       arbitration under clause 25 below.

   (c) The Publishers shall not reject the script for any
       reason other than its failure to meet the specifications
       in (a) above.

(d)   Should the Author fail to meet the delivery date
      specified, the Publishers may give the Author six months'
      notice in writing to deliver the work and should he fail
      to do so the Publishers shall be entitled to terminate
      the contract in which event any advance shall be
      returnable and all rights shall revert to the Author.

2.   Warranty & Indemnity

The Author shall warrant that the work is an original work,
that it has not been published within the territories in which
exclusive rights have been granted to the Publishers by the
contract, that it does not infringe any existing copyright,
and that to the best of the Author's knowledge and ability it
contains nothing libellous or defamatory.

The Author shall indemnify the Publishers against any loss
injury or damage resulting from any breach by the Author
(unknown to the Publishers) of the warranty, provided that any
legal costs and expenses and any compensation, damages, costs
and disbursements shall be paid by the Publishers only on the
joint advice of the respective legal advisers of the Author
and the Publishers and failing agreement on the advice of
Counsel selected and instructed jointly on behalf of the
Publishers and the Author. The extent of the Author's indemnity
shall not exceed the total monies received by the Author under
the contract.

3.   Copyright Fees & Index

(a)   The Publishers shall pay any copyright fees for
      illustrations and/or quotations up to a maximum of £
      any further sum being paid by the Publishers but deducted
      from the Author's royalties.

(b)   If in the opinion of the Author and the Publishers an
      index is required but the Author does not wish to
      undertake the task, the Publishers shall engage a competent
      indexer to do so and the costs shall be shared equally
      between the Author and the Publishers, the Author's share
      being deducted from royalties.

4.   Licence

The copyright in the work shall remain the property of the
Author who shall grant to the Publishers the sole and exclusive
right for a period of ten years from the date of the contract
or delivery of the script (whichever is the later) to print,
publish and sell the work in volume form and to sub-license
such rights specified in Clauses 13, 14, 15, 16 and 17 (a)
hereof as may be agreed in the contract. Except in the case of
anthology and quotation rights, if the Publishers wish to enter
into any such sub-licence, they shall obtain the consent of the
Author (such consent not to be unreasonably withheld or delayed),
supplying him with a copy of the sub-licence before it is signed.
If the work is in print (as defined in Clause 23 (b) hereof) at
the end of ten years after delivery of the typescript, the
Publishers shall have first refusal to enter into a further
contract with the Author.

5.   Publishers' Undertaking to Publish

Provided that the work meets the specification in Clause 1(a)
above, the Publishers shall publish the work at their own

expense and risk in a first edition consisting of the number
of copies named in approximate terms in the contract within
twelve months (unless otherwise agreed in writing) of delivery
of the typescript and any other material specified in
accordance with Clause 1. Should the Publishers fail to
comply with their undertaking, the advance stipulated in Clause
10 hereof (or any balance unpaid) shall be paid to the Author
together with such additional amount as may be awarded under
Clause 25 hereof as compensation for such failure by the
Publishers.

6. Production

   (a)   All details as to the manner of production and publication
         and the number and destination of free copies shall be
         under the control of the Publishers who undertake to
         produce the book to a high standard.

   (b)   The Publishers shall obtain the Author's approval of copy
         editing, blurb, catalogue copy, number and type of
         illustrations, jacket design and publication date, such
         approval not to be unreasonably withheld or delayed.

   (c)   No changes in the title or text shall be made by the
         Publishers without the Author's written consent.

   (d)   Within ten days of publication the Publishers shall inform
         the Author of the number of copies printed and the number
         and destination of free copies distributed.

   (e)   Within thirty days of publication the Publishers shall
         return to the Author the typescript of the work.

   (f)   The Publishers shall ensure that the provisions contained
         in (b) and (c) above are included in any contract for
         sub-licensed editions of the work in the English language.

7. Approval of Final Edited Script and Correction of Proofs

   (a)   The Author shall be sent for approval a copy of the final
         edited script at least 14 days before it goes to the
         printers.

   (b)   The Author shall be sent two complete sets of proofs of
         the work and proofs of the illustrations and captions and
         notes on the jacket. The Author shall correct and return
         one set of proofs to the Publishers within 14 days.
         The Author shall bear the cost of proof corrections
         (other than printers' or Publishers' errors) in excess
         of 15% of the cost of composition, such cost to be
         deducted from royalties.

8. Marketing

   The Publishers shall use their best endeavours to market the
   work effectively and shall, in particular, despatch review
   copies at least one month before the publication date, include
   and describe correctly the work in their catalogue, and do
   everything they reasonably can to ensure that copies are ready
   for sale in all leading bookshops by publication day.

9. Copyright Notice and Credit to the Author

   A copyright notice in the form © followed by the Author's
   name and the year of publication shall be printed on all copies
   of the work and the Author's name shall appear prominently on

the jacket, binding and title page of the work and in all publicity material. The Publishers shall ensure that an identical copyright notice appears in all sub-licensed editions of the work.

10. Advance

(a) The Publishers shall pay the Author an advance against royalties which shall be calculated as follows :

(i) On account of the publishers' own editions: not less than 65% of the Author's estimated receipts from the sale of the projected first printing (if the Publishers' turnover is not less than £   per annum); and

(ii) On account of any rights granted under clauses 13, 14, 15 & 16: a sum additional to that under (i) above, to be negotiated between the Author and the Publishers and to be itemised separately both in the contract and the account statements rendered to the Author.

(b) In the case of a non-commissioned work half the advance shall be paid on signature of the contract and half within one year of signature or on publication, whichever is the sooner.

(c) In the case of a commissioned work the advance shall be paid either

(i) one third on signature of the contract
one third on delivery of the typescript and
one third within one year of delivery of the typescript
or on publication whichever is the sooner; or

(ii) one half on signature of the contract and
one half on delivery of the typescript.

(d) Except in the case of termination of the contract pursuant to clause 1 (d) above, the advance shall be non returnable and shall be paid in full.

(e) Within ten days of publication the Publishers shall pay to the Author such sum as may be required to bring the advance payment up to the 65% of the Author's receipts from the sale of the entire first printing.

11. Royalties

(a) On home market sales in the UK and Irish Republic and on overseas sales at discounts of less than 45%

10% of the British published price on the first 2,500 copies, 12½% on the next 2,500 copies, and 15% thereafter.

(b) On overseas sales (other than to the USA) at discounts of 45% or more

5% of the British published price on the first 2,500 copies, 6¼% on the next 2,500 copies, and 7½% thereafter.

(c) English language editions published overseas (other than US editions)

The Publishers shall pay to the Author a royalty to be agreed on all copies of any edition in the English language produced and published outside the United Kingdom (other than the USA) either by themselves or by arrangement with another publisher.

(d) Reduced royalties shall not be paid on any reprint unless otherwise agreed in writing.

(e) No proportion of royalties due to the Author shall be reserved against return copies.

(f) Cheap and other hardback editions
The Publishers shall pay to the Author a royalty to be agreed on any hardback edition published at less than two-thirds of the original published price and also on any "special" hardback edition under their imprint, e.g. an educational or large print edition.

12. Remainders & Surplus Stock

If not less than two years after first publication the Publishers

(a) wish to sell off copies at a reduced price or as a remainder; or

(b) wish to destroy surplus bound copies

they shall notify the Author accordingly. In the case of (a) the Publishers shall pay the Author 10% of the net receipts and shall give him the option to purchase copies at the remainder price. In the case of (b) the Author shall have the right to obtain free copies within 28 days of the notification.

13. Paperbacks

(a) Should the Publishers publish a paperback edition under their own imprint or under that of an associated company they shall pay to the Author on all sales in the home market & overseas including the USA 7½% of the British published price on the first 20,000 copies and 10% thereafter.

(b) Should the Publishers sub-license paperback rights to an independent paperback publisher, all monies accruing under such sub-licence shall be divided in the proportion 60% to the Author 40% to the Publishers on the first £5,000 accruing under the sub-licence, and 70% to the Author and 30% to the Publishers thereafter.

14. Bookclub and Digest Rights

Should the Publishers sub-license simultaneous or reprint book-club rights or the right of condensation in volume form they shall pay the Author as follows:

(a) On bound copies or sheets sold to the bookclub:

50% of net receipts (being the difference between the sale price and the cost of manufacture) up to £5,000 and 60% on all receipts thereafter. In the event of such a sale the Publishers shall inform the Author of the gross amount received from the bookclub and the cost of manufacture.

(b) On copies manufactured by the bookclub:
60% of the Publishers' receipts up to £5,000 and 70% thereafter

(c) On copies sold to a bookclub owned or partly owned by the Publishers or one of their associated companies:
7½% of the bookclub price.

15. <u>United States Rights</u>

    (a)   If the Author grants to the Publishers US rights in the work, they shall make every effort to arrange the publication of an American edition of the work on a royalty basis. The Publishers shall retain not more than 15% of the proceeds from any such edition inclusive of any sub-agent's commission. Should the Publishers fail to negotiate publication of an American edition on a royalty basis, but obtain an offer for an edition at a price inclusive of the Author's remuneration, they shall pay the Author not less than 12½% of their net receipts.

    (b)   If the Author retains US rights but the Publishers agree to act as his agent for the sale of these rights, US publication shall be covered by a separate contract between the Author and the American publishers. The Publishers shall retain as an agency commission not more than 15% of the proceeds from any such edition inclusive of any sub-agent's commission.

16. <u>Translation Rights</u>

    (a)   If the Author grants to the Publishers translation rights in the work, they shall retain not more than 20% of the proceeds from any foreign language edition inclusive of any sub-agent's commission.

    (b)   If the Author retains translation rights but the Publishers agree to act as his agent for the sale of these rights, any foreign-language edition of the work shall be covered by a separate contract between the Author and the foreign-language publishers. The Publishers shall retain as an agency commission not more than 20% of the proceeds from any such edition inclusive of any sub-agent's commission.

17. <u>Subsidiary Rights</u>

    (a)   If the Author grants to the Publishers an exclusive licence to handle the following rights on his behalf the Publishers shall pay to the Author the following percentages of the proceeds:

(i)	Second, i.e. post volume publication serial rights	80%
(ii)	Anthology & quotation rights	60%
(iii)	Condensation rights	75%
(iv)	Strip cartoon rights	75%

    (b)   The following rights shall be expressly reserved for the Author together with any rights not specified above:

       First serial, one-shot periodical, film and dramatic, TV and radio dramatisation, TV and radio readings, reprography, merchandising, video and sound recording, Public Lending.

18. <u>Author's Copies</u>

The Author shall receive on publication 12 presentation copies of the work and shall have the right to purchase further copies at the lowest trade price for personal use.

Should a paperback edition be issued under Clause 13 (a), the Author shall be entitled to 20 presentation copies.

19. Accounts

(a) The Publishers shall make up accounts at six monthly intervals and shall render such accounts and pay all monies due to the Author within three months thereof.

(b) Monies due to the Author under either Clause 10(a) (i) or Clause 10(a) (ii) shall not be withheld on account of an unearned advance under the other of these two sub-clauses. Any sum of £100 or more due to the Author in respect of sub-licensed rights shall be paid to the Author within one month of receipt provided the advance under Clause 10(a)(ii) has been earned.

(c) Each statement of account shall report the number of copies printed, the number of free copies distributed, the number of copies sold during the previous accounting period, the total sales to date, the list price, the royalty rate, the amount of royalties, the number of returned copies, the gross amount received pursuant to each licence granted by the Publishers, and itemized deductions. Each statement of account shall be accompanied by copies of statements received from sub-licensed publishers.

(d) The Publishers shall make no deductions from monies due to the Author other than those provided for herein. In the event of late payment, the Publishers shall pay interest on monies overdue at the rate of 3% above the base rate of the major clearing banks.

(e) The Author or his authorised representative shall have the right upon written request to examine the Publishers' books of account in so far as they relate to the work, which examination shall be at the cost of the Author unless errors exceeding 2% of the total sums paid to the Author shall be found to his disadvantage in which case the costs shall be paid by the Publishers.

20. Actions for Infringement

If either the Author or the Publishers consider the copyright in the work has been infringed both parties shall join in any legal proceedings and the party initiating such proceedings shall pay all costs and expenses and indemnify the other. Any monies which shall be recovered in respect of any such infringement of copyright shall after deduction of all costs and expenses be divided equally between the Author and the Publishers.

21. Revised Editions

The work shall not be revised or re-issued in altered or expanded form without the Author's consent. If the Author and the Publishers agree that the Author shall undertake revisions or provide new material for a new edition, this work shall be undertaken subject to an agreed advance against royalties being paid to the Author. No third party shall be engaged to revise or add to the work without the Author's written consent.

22. Assignment

The Publishers shall not assign the rights granted to them in the contract or the benefit thereof without the Author's written consent.

23. Termination

(a) If the Publishers fail to fulfil or comply with any of the provisions of the contract within one month after notification from the Author of such failure or if they go into liquidation or have a Receiver appointed, the contract shall automatically terminate and all rights granted by it shall revert to the Author.

(b) If after all editions of the work published under their own imprint are out of print or off the market the Publishers have not within six months of a written request from the Author issued a new edition or impression of at least 1,500 copies (unless a lesser number of copies be mutually agreed) the contract shall terminate and all rights granted shall revert to the Author. The work shall be considered to be out of print for the purposes of the contract if fewer than 12 copies of an edition under the Publishers' imprint are shown to have been sold in any statement of account or if fewer than 50 copies remain in stock.

Termination under (a) or (b) shall be without prejudice to:

(i) any sub-licences properly granted by the Publishers during the currency of the contract, and

(ii) any claims which the Author may have for monies due at the time of such termination, and

(iii) any claims which the Author may have against the Publishers in respect of breaches by the Publishers of the terms of the contract.

24. Advertisements

The Publishers and the publishers of any sub-licensed edition shall not insert within the work or on its cover or dust jacket any advertisement other than for their own works without the Author's consent.

25. Disputes

Any dispute arising in connection with the contract shall be referred to a joint committee composed of a representative of the Society of Authors, a representative of the Writers' Guild and two representatives appointed by the Publishers but not connected with their company, whose unanimous decision shall be binding. Failing unanimous agreement, the dispute shall be referred to a single arbitrator appointed by the above named parties and the decision of the arbitrator shall be binding. Failing agreement on the choice of a single arbitrator, the dispute shall be referred to the London Court of Arbitration under its rules.

26. Option

The Author shall not grant the Publishers an option or first refusal on any of his future works.

APPENDIX A.   PAPERBACK AGREEMENT

Where the work is originally published in paperback form by the
Publishers the minimum terms and conditions shall be the same as
those set out in the hardcover Agreement except that the following
clauses shall be substituted :

Clause 11. Royalties

(a)   on all sales in the home market and overseas including
      the USA

      7½% of the British published price on the first 20,000
      copies and 10% of the British published price thereafter.

(b)   reduced royalties shall not be paid on any reprint unless
      otherwise agreed in writing.

(c)   no proportion of royalties due to the Author shall be
      reserved against return copies.

Clause 13. Hardcover Editions

(a)   Should the Publishers publish a hardcover edition under their
      own imprint or under that of an associated company the
      Publishers shall pay to the Author the following royalties:

      (i)   on home market sales in the UK and Irish Republic and
            on overseas sales at discounts of less than 45%

            10% of the British published price on the first 2,500
            copies, 12½% on the next 2,500 copies, and 15%
            thereafter.

      (ii) on overseas sales (other than the USA) at discounts of
            45% or more

            5% of the British published price on the first 2,500
            copies, 6¼% on the next 2,500 copies, and 7½%
            thereafter.

(b)   Should the Publishers sub-license hardcover rights to an
      independent hardcover publisher, all monies accruing under
      such a sub-licence shall be divided in the proportion 80%
      to the Author and 20% to the Publishers.

CLAUSES IN THE CONTRACT

The Minimum Terms Agreement more or less speaks for itself. But as it is not in general use yet, my students are always asking me what terms to look for when they receive an average contract. Could we look at some of these in more detail?

THE ADVANCE

The advance is an expression used for money which an author may keep no matter how well or badly his book sells. It is supposed to be based on the number of copies a publisher hopes to sell. For convenience, let us suppose the publisher hopes to sell 2,500 copies at a selling price of £10. As an author's normal percentage of the retail price is 10 per cent, he would in theory receive £2,500 if all the books sold.

His publisher, however, knows it is most unusual for a first novel to sell as many as 2,500 and as business works on the practice of taking chances only with the other man's money, he will in all likelihood halve that figure and advance the writer £1,250. That, incidentally, would be quite a generous publisher - many would make it far less. (Indeed I have been told there are publishers in this country who are actually paying no more than £100 for a full length novel which might have taken its author a year to complete. It is quite true. The days of slavery are not over!)

But let us return to our generous publisher. Even he does not pay the author his advance of £1,250 in one sum. The practice is to pay half of the advance on signature of the contract and the second half on the day of publication. As few books in Britain ever come out less than a year after acceptance, it will be noted by the more cynical among us that even our honest publisher is not unaware of the advantages he gains from inflation.

So the author would receive £625 on acceptance and £625 on publication. This represents the royalties on 1,250 books and the writer will receive no more money until this number has sold: that is until the publisher has recovered his advance money from the author's ten per cent royalties. Only after that point will the writer begin to receive his £1 per book.

But wait, the publisher only collates his sales figures every six months. Collates, not pays. The writer has to wait another three months after that collation for his royalties. That would apply to a good publisher. As already stated a frightening number of publishers go well beyond their contract dates before paying their authors. It will be appreciated now why a writer should always wear his tin hat when he emerges into the business world.

SUB-LICENSED SALES

A writer should make certain the sub-licensed sales clause is fair and just. Hardcover publishers insist on a share of paperback sales these days but in my view they are never entitled to more than 40 per cent from such a sale, although they will nearly always demand 50 per cent. Whichever figure is accepted, it should be scaled down rapidly once the paperback sales have gone over 25,000 copies.

SERIAL RIGHTS

Other sub-licensed sales include first serial rights to a national magazine. This sale can happen before or after book publication. If it happens before, a publisher has no claim to a percentage. If it happens after publication, a publisher is likely to claim 50 per cent of the money received because he will argue, with some justification, that if he had not published the book in the first place, the magazine buying the story might never have heard of it.

FOREIGN TRANSLATIONS

A writer should watch the clause dealing with foreign translations. Strictly speaking a publisher has no claim whatever to a share in foreign sales but these days more and more are demanding a cut of them. If they insist, 10 per cent should be an author's maximum concession.

RECORDING AND VISUAL RIGHTS

The following rights should be expressly reserved for the author: one-shot periodical, film and dramatic, television and radio dramatisation, television and radio readings, reprography, merchandising, video and sound recording, electronic rights and Public Lending.

GOING OUT OF PRINT

Remember to insist on a clause that ensures a writer is notified before his book is remaindered. The period should not, normally, be less than two years from first publication. This clause should also give the author the opportunity to buy any books he needs at the remaindered price.

Linked to this clause, is that of contract termination. This allows the author to recover rights quickly if the book goes out of print, if the sales figures fall below a reasonable number, and/or if the publisher fails to comply with the publication terms of the contract or goes into liquidation.

COPYRIGHT CLAIM

There should be a clause obliging the publisher to print the author's copyright claim in the flyleaf of the book.

MORAL RIGHTS

An author is legally entitled to the two basic rights of paternity and integrity. The first is his right to be identified as the author of a work, and the second is the right to prevent any distortion of it that would prejudice his reputation.

Under the Copyright, Designs and Patents Act 1988, the assertion of moral rights of paternity should be done in writing via the contract. A suggested clause would read: 'The author asserts his moral rights to be identified as the author of the work in relation to all such rights as are granted by the author to the publisher under the terms and conditions of this contract.'

A publisher, or any sub-licensee, should print a statement to this effect on the verso title page of every edition of the book.

Moral rights of integrity do not have to be asserted, though both rights may be waived, should the author so wish. Once waived, rights cannot be reclaimed and an author should not agree to waive rights of paternity without legal consultation.

As with copyright, moral rights can be passed on at death, usually to the copyright holder, unless specified otherwise in the author's will.

OPTION CLAUSES

Authors should resist, if possible, the inclusion of a clause entitling a publisher to right of first refusal on a subsequent book. However, this may not prove possible, particularly with a first novel by an unknown writer, as the publisher would wish to share in any future success, having taken the initial financial risk.

If an option clause is to be included, it should be strictly limited to one book, at terms to be mutually agreed. It should not, under any circumstances, provide for publication of a subsequent book on the same terms as the current work to which the contract relates.

Although an option clause is, therefore, an expression of continued interest on a publisher's part, an author is free, if he feels the subsequent offer made by the publisher is too low, to reject it in favour of a more advantageous one.

As no one can reasonably expect to obtain a perfect contract, it is obviously in the author's interest to assure for himself the most favourable terms he can. Would you agree that any contract should be most carefully considered bearing in mind the clauses we have just listed?

Those listed are the main clauses, although as the Minimum Terms Agreement shows, there are others that should be included for the security of both parties. However, if my advice has been taken and a good agent has been called in, he should give the contract a thorough vetting himself. Even so, a novice should remember my warning about inefficiency and not rely entirely upon his agent's scrutiny. A writer should compare the contract himself alongside the MTA and if he feels some important clause is omitted, he should bring it to the agent's or publisher's attention. It will not offend either of them if he does this: indeed they will respect him for having a business head on his shoulders. And it could save him both money and problems in the months and years ahead.

It would do no harm to reiterate at this point that if the novice joined either The Writers' Guild or The Society of Authors, he could have his contract vetted by them free of charge.

22 *The Pros and Cons of Writing for a Career*

From your experience, what advice would you give a writer who has just sold his first book?

I would repeat my warning not to be tempted to give up his job at this stage. One book, even two or three books, seldom spell security in such a fickle profession. I know I went against my own advice thirty-six years ago but insanity isn't something one wants to pass on to others.

I'll go even further than this and say that I don't believe any man or woman whose only aim is to make money should go in for writing novels at all. Money can be made a hundred times more easily in a thousand other jobs. The truth is that the average financial return for novelists is pathetic for the work involved.

I know there is always the possibility of a best-seller but so there is the possibility of getting twelve draws in the football pools or winning a lottery. Frankly, I wouldn't put the odds much higher. In these days of media pressure and public acquiescence, for a book to become a best-seller it needs massive hype from its publisher and hype of that magnitude happens to only one book in ten thousand.

The same applies to the sale of other rights. At one time the big film studios used to employ readers whose sole job was to read every new book that was published. With the demise of the big studios, this is no longer the practice. It follows, therefore, that unless a novel has gained a big name from the advertising spent on it, it is unlikely to be noticed by television and film producers.

Unless, that is, the author knows his share of critics and producers. In that case the odd word here and there will do more good than a hundred submissions sent in by an unknown scribe.

So it's the old story, who you know, not what you know? Or in this case, not how well you write but having good connections?

If someone asked me to draw up a list of the qualities an author needs to get into television or films (where the real money is) I would put the producers and directors he knows at the head of the list and talent little more than halfway down. Those novices who have attended writers' conferences might have heard much the same from other writers (allowing that those writers have given an honest talk and not tried to butter up their audience). For that matter, one has only to watch a few of the mini-series dished up on television to realise that quality and talent were the last assets demanded when the book or script was bought.

With publishers, the name on the spine of the book is the thing. The novice will soon find that no matter how brilliant his latest book, his publisher will give it the merest whisper beside the publicity he gives to the tired work of one of his big-name authors.

This can irritate if the established writer is clearly past his best. What is worse is when a well-known pop star, politician, or even a big-time racketeer, decides to write a novel (aided in most cases by a ghost writer to give the work shape and substance). Although the book can be, and usually is, an inferior work, the talented novice will find most or all of his publisher's monthly marketing budget goes into its promotion, leaving our real novelist with a book no one hears about.

This really ought not to surprise anyone. We are talking about business and isn't it true that rewards in business so often depend on favouritism, nepotism, or impressive names on company letterheads? Perhaps in the final analysis we, the reading public, deserve what we get for our lack of discernment.

It would seem from your somewhat bleak picture of the profession that you would discourage the putting of pen to paper. Given your long and successful career, you can't really hold such a view, can you?

I believe, and have always believed, that it is wrong, and even dishonest, not to tell would-be writers the truth. Writing is one of the cruellest professions in the world, and if a would-be author has the kind of temperament that rages when inferior talent is given preference over his work, then such a man should not enter the profession because it will happen to him so often that his arteries will not stand the strain.

Nor is there much loyalty shown these days. An author might contribute as many as half a dozen novels to a publisher and bring the company in a good deal of money. Then suddenly, sometimes without a word of explanation, he may be dropped from the publisher's list, usually because a new policy has been determined at the top or because of a takeover. I don't exaggerate because this has happened to me. These are the debit sides to the profession and I believe it is only right to state them.

But there is a credit side too, so let us concentrate on that. All these odds can be defeated if a beginner has the dedication to face the inequity and disappointments of the profession, and the stubbornness not to be defeated. I have managed to live and raise a family entirely on my work and it would be unfair to my profession not to admit it. And when I began I knew nobody in the trade, not an editor, not an agent, not even another writer. What I have done, others have done, and beginners can do the same, even if we accept the fact that a private path to certain offices would hasten our progress.

We *can* manage without anyone's favours. And in an odd convoluted way, our very weakness in having no arms to support us gives us a strength they do not have. Whenever I get depressed, I recall something that happened to me many years ago.

I was walking with a friend of mine, another freelance writer, down Fleet Street. We had both had novels recently rejected and were feeling very sorry for ourselves. In fact we were wondering why we were such fools to be writers when there was so much more money, power and prestige in publishing.

This mood had come about from our having lunch with an acquaintance who had recently been given an editorial directorship in a publishing house and who was reeking with money and self-gratification.

We tramped along gloomily for a while until my friend rallied and turned to me. "You know, there is one thing on our side, F E. At least we're not at the mercy of shareholders or takeover bids. I mean we can always work, can't we?"

I was not to be comforted. "You mean we can always write more books? Even when no publisher accepts them?"

His smile faded and he sighed. "True," he said. "Too true."

Yet six months later, our acquaintance's publishing house was taken over and he lost his job while we, after still more rejections, sold our novels and were in business again.

The author must have broad shoulders and considerable tenacity if he's to make his mark in spite of the odds. Would you add to that a measure of self-confidence in his own work?

Yes, he must have that. He must believe in himself, his work, and his profession. It is not always easy, particularly when haughty agents or publishers try to undermine his confidence. If he is convinced their criticisms are not valid - and he should always check that first - then he should remember what was said earlier in this book. Authors are the bedrock of the entire literary profession. Without us the castles of agents and publishers alike slide into the sea. We are the only indispensables because we are the creators, and without being opinionated or arrogant, we should never let them or ourselves forget it.

Part Three

Miscellanea

**All the things you wanted to know: but didn't
know where to ask.**

**In this section, both authors draw on their considerable experience,
Frederick E Smith (F E S) as a novelist, Moe Sherrard-Smith (M S S)
as an assessor and tutor, to offer personal opinion and advice on a
number of subjects not covered in the text but of vital importance
to the would-be author.**

AUTHORS - BORN OR MADE?

F E S
I believe they are born because of the assorted qualities an author
needs. (Not necessarily admirable qualities, let me hastily add, but
qualities required by the discipline.) These include an instinctive
sense of drama, a highly developed imagination, an inquisitive
intellect, a self-critical disposition, a character that can take punishment, and an ability to work alone for long periods.

Although some of these qualities can be learned and developed,
others can never be. That is why throughout this book we have
emphasised the need for a beginner to be self-critical, and never to
attempt a career as a writer until he has proved to himself beyond
doubt that he has the necessary stamina and qualifications.

M S S
In a sense he is both born and made, since an author is an
amalgam of parts. Any person, reasonably fluent in his own language, can be 'made' a writer by being taught the rudiments of
techniques necessary to suit various media.

But unless that same person was 'born' with the story-teller's gift,
he may become a fairly competent producer of the written word in
fields such as articles, but he will not succeed in becoming a
novelist. That degree of imaginative creative skill is, I am
convinced, inherent.

ACCEPTING COMMISSIONS

F E S

For a beginner, it is obviously a huge encouragement for an editor to commission work from him. But he must not allow this interest to go to his head. He should remember that an editor's interest is one thing and a firm commitment is another. Too often authors are encouraged to write lengthy scripts, only to be told when the work is finished that the person who initiated the project has changed his mind and the deal is off.

It is true that this happens more in television and films than in the book and magazine world, but nevertheless it does happen far too frequently in all four. Ideally, a writer ought to be given either a financial advance before starting the work (called front money) or a contract that guarantees him some payment if the deal falls through. If he is offered no guarantee and still decides to write the work, then he must face the possibility of wasting X number of weeks or months on a work that might never see the light of day. It is something that has happened to most of us and it isn't an easy thing to accept. So be warned.

BLURBS

F E S

These are the potted synopses one sees on the inside flaps of book jackets and sometimes on the flyleaves of the book itself. Quite often a publisher asks an author to write the blurb himself. In other cases he has it written by a member of his staff and gives the author the opportunity to make any amendments he sees fit.

Blurbs for novels are difficult things to write because they are usually limited to between 150 and 200 words and within those limits must give a brief outline of the book's contents without giving away the plot. They must also be written in such a way they will tempt a would-be reader to buy or borrow the book.

To authors who are given the opportunity to write their own blurbs, a word of warning might not come amiss here. Just as book jackets are, in my opinion, losing the public's confidence by their indiscriminate use of sex, so blurbs by using absurd superlatives are producing the same effect. Far better to let the quality of the book be evident through the skill and construction of the blurb. When integrity is brought back into the book trade, both authors and publishers will benefit.

BOOKSHELF CATEGORISATION

M S S

The growing tendency for accountants and sales managers to control the marketing of books is leading to greater pressure on authors to conform to genre labelling. This is a deplorable practice, and one authors ought to resist whenever possible.

Agreed, there are writers whose books are in specialities such as crime, westerns, or science fiction, and they can rightly be so categorised. Apart from that, why is every author being squeezed into an artificial category in which he may lie an uneasy bedfellow? Is romance really so different from historical romance? Or historical fiction from the thriller, if all are competently written?

The 'general fiction' category should be one open to all types of book outside the three previously mentioned. If not, the danger is - as already exists - that at best an author does not become familiar to regular fans as his books are scattered throughout the shelves in various arbitrary categories. At worst, excellent novels could be rejected by publishers because such books do not fit neatly into these slots or because authors refuse to conform.

CLOSED SHOP FOR WRITERS?

M S S

Is writing a closed shop? It might seem from some comments throughout this book that, if not closed, the entrance mechanism is fairly tight.

And yet, a good book will almost certainly be published. Of course there are mistakes. Publishers like the rest of us are human and occasionally fallible. But mistakes apart, there is no bar to entrance into the world of authorship.

It has, in many senses, a greater equality of opportunity than exists in the office workplace, in that books by men and women have the same chance of publication.

The one drawback that will effectively create a closed shop is the flooding of publishing houses with badly written and patently unpublishable manuscripts. This can only be avoided by would-be writers cultivating the quality stressed in many parts of this book - totally ruthless and objective self-criticism.

Those would-be writers who have not this facility and send out a manuscript in the belief that 'it might not be quite right but it will do' are the enemies of all concerned.

COMPUTER DISCS v MANUSCRIPT

F E S

As progress can't be stopped, there's no doubt that more and more publishers are going to ask authors to submit their work on word processor discs instead of on paper. Equally, once they have experienced how easy amendments and corrections are to make on PCWs, more writers are going to prefer this method.

At the same time, many writers find it difficult to work only on a PCW. The problem comes from remembering what one has said previously. If the manuscript is typed out, it is comparatively easy to refer back to an earlier chapter. On a PCW this might mean changing a disc and then running page after page up on the screen before one finds the relevant paragraph.

Another problem lies in checking individual words. Some writers find it more difficult to spot errors on the screen than on printed paper although, of course, spelling checks are now available for machines.

A final problem has already been mentioned. Errors that a printer should spot on a manuscript are more likely to slip unnoticed into the published book if only a PCW disc is used.

My personal answer to these problems is to print out a manuscript from the discs and then, after making any final corrections on the MS, amend the discs accordingly. I then send both manuscript and discs to the publisher.

One final word about providing a publisher with discs. As he is saving money by having them to print from, he ought to give a percentage of his savings to the author. I believe it should be no less than fifty per cent but no doubt the writers' guilds will soon be issuing guidelines on this matter.

M S S

Because of a computer's similarity to the more familiar typewriter, in having a keyboard, many writers think they are the same. But with the keyboard the similarity ends. The word processor package of a computer (the PCW) can do so much more, and in different ways.

Unlike the old typewriter which produced a one-off page, or even the electronic typewriters which have a relatively small memory, the PCW stores the manuscript on discs, usually 3″, 3½″ or 5¼″ floppy discs (occasionally on hard disc, for the more adept and wealthy users) for future use. This allows the editing of text with consummate ease, which relieves the burden of laboriously re-typing a page on the old manual Remington, or re-numbering the entire script.

The biggest advantage in using a word processor is that a neatly-presented and uniform typescript can be prepared ready for submission. No more excuses for dog-eared scripts and endless crossings-out. A script which has pages creased or disfigured by a series of unsuccessful submissions to publishers can, in a matter of moments, have those pages re-typed almost effortlessly.

Before submitting discs to a publisher it will be necessary to find out whether your system is compatible with his system. If not, you may be faced with finding a friendly computer supplier who can configure the information (perhaps on a larger disc via an interface) in acceptable form.

You should also submit a print-out of your keyboard, so that a copy editor can readily decipher the stroke you meant and/or the codes inserted.

COPYRIGHT PERMISSIONS

F E S

If a writer wishes to use a lengthy extract from another author's work he must always ask that author's permission and should obtain it in writing. If he does not get this permission, he is infringing copyright.

Although ideally he should ask permission in every case, it is not considered necessary if he is only quoting a line or two of another man's work. Even so, he should always make mention of that writer's name.

A less defined area is entered when an author uses other writers' books for research. He might not repeat the text of these works in his own book - which makes infringement of copyrights very difficult or even impossible to prove - and yet the substance of his book might be based partly or even entirely on the items that the other writers have researched and published. In such cases integrity and courtesy demand that an author gives full and generous credit to his benefactors in the flyleaves of his work.

GENDER WRITING

M S S

A novelist isn't going to be successful at his craft if he can't put himself into the mind and persona of each character he creates. Whether that character is male or female is, then, irrelevant.

As said Shylock in the Merchant of Venice: *"If you prick us, do we not bleed? if you tickle us do we not laugh? if you poison us, do we not die? and if you wrong us, shall we not revenge? If we are like you in the rest, we will resemble you in that."* Whilst he spoke of the homogenous brotherhood of Jews and Christians, his reflections could apply equally to gender in writing. The emotions of men and women are essentially the same, although the outward expression of them may differ.

Though a woman writer myself, the majority of my successful stories have been written from the man's point of view, putting myself in the shoes and mind of a male character. I have never perceived any problem in so doing. Writing from the opposite sex's standpoint does not, in any way, diminish one's own sexuality - a criticism often hurled at male authors writing through a woman's eyes. On the contrary, it should be viewed as a more imaginative facet of the author's talent.

What is necessary for the writer is to imagine the character in the round before putting pen to paper. This will enable him to visualise the other sex's emotions and responses, which in turn will bring the character to life.

F E S

I agree with all that M S S has said, certainly as far as straight novels are concerned. It is not difficult to see the world through the opposite sex's eyes provided one allows for the physiological differences between man and woman, and a good imaginative writer can soon train himself to do this. The result, without compromise to either sex, will be novels that satisfy men and women alike.

Mind you, I must be absolutely honest here and admit that a lack of this ability does not necessarily condemn a novelist to oblivion. Dickens' women were the most implausible of creatures and yet his other qualities more than compensated for them. Nevertheless, even his novels would have been improved by more realistic females, and for lesser mortals the ability to draw believable male and female characters will greatly improve their work and make it popular to both sexes.

In these cases, whatever the subject and whether the novel's main characters are female or male, the style will remain the same. However, when genre novels enter the field, the situation changes quite dramatically. A publisher of gentle romances would hardly be likely to take a novel written in the terse, graphic style of a war novel, and vice versa. Although we all know that some women like masculine-type novels and some men like romances, convention demands that novels specifically aimed at one or the other use a different style and vocabulary. One feels that as female emancipation grows that these differences might narrow, but until they do, the genre writer must take note of them. At the same time, none of this prohibits a man writing romances or a woman writing gritty thrillers. The essentials are commonsense and a sound imagination.

GHOST WRITERS

F E S

These are the unrecognised writers who fill out and shape the jottings of anyone from pop stars to politicians who, by themselves, are incapable of turning out readable text. Ghost writers are employed by newspapers, publishers, and sometimes by the 'big names' themselves who, without them, would not be able to command the large fees they obtain.

Although the practice is rampant today, I dislike it for a number of reasons, one being its effect on the writing profession. When the man in the street sees some half-literate sportsman turning out a well-crafted book or weekly newspaper articles, the effect is to make him believe how easy professional writing must be. This in turn leads to a further flooding of the limited market by people who are no more capable of writing than the celebrities themselves.

Although I've nothing but sympathy for writers who, for various reasons, are compelled to make a living this way, my sympathy does not extend to the people who use them without giving them full credit for their contribution. While to do this might defeat the purpose of using a ghost, which is to elevate further the standing of the celebrity, nevertheless I find it despicable that people can take full credit for another man's work in this way. One wonders how these people can bear to see their names heading such material in the newspapers or on their own bookshelves.

M S S
There is a very fine line to be drawn between editing and ghosting in a short work. But when a major re-write has been done (as in many so-called autobiographies), it would be more honest to say 'The story of Joe Bloggs, *as told to* Jim Brown' - that way the real author gets full credit.

INHIBITIONS

M S S
If a novelist's own inhibitions won't let him write about certain matters, say religious persecution or homosexuality, then he will have consciously to choose a genre in which neither element is likely to occur. And he will then find that he cannot step outside those boundaries for fear the forbidden subjects cross his path. If the writer is happy to operate within those restrictions, then so be it. Yet a vital spark may well be missing from his work, as a certain reticence will always keep him teetering on the brink of self-expression, without ever taking the plunge.

But the creative and imaginative writer has to accept that he should mirror life in its widest possible spectrum. In that sense, if his writing is to make an important contribution to literature then, within the boundaries of good taste, his own inhibitions should be firmly locked in the closet for the duration of his writing stint.

The inhibitions of one's family and friends should likewise not be allowed to intrude. *They* are not writing the book, *they* are not creating the characters. If they do not like the end product, then they can decline to read it. If they are embarrassed, they can decline to discuss it. Allowing them to dictate the content is as much a form of censorship as any other. Writers have met untimely deaths defending just such a right of free expression.

F E S
Apart from personal inhibitions which M S S has discussed fully, close relationships can be a great handicap to a sensitive writer. His book might need a tender passage but he feels if he writes it his colleagues at work might make fun of him. His book needs a passionate love scene but he is afraid his wife might think the scene is drawn from an experience with another woman or that he is expressing in words something his marriage is denying him.

One could go on and on with these inhibitions and there is only one answer to them all. If a man wants to be a writer, he must not allow others to dictate the substance of his book, *unless* he is writing an autobiography or some such factual work. In such cases he may be forced to impose some restrictions on himself, to save others pain or to avoid libel actions.

But if he is writing fiction and he wants to get power and authority into his work, he has no option but to put into it the scenes and the ideas that it needs. If in doing this he reveals aspects of his personality his wife and friends never suspected, so be it. In most cases little or no damage will be done. The writer might even discover his wife and friends find him a more interesting person than they did before.

But whatever the effects, inhibitions must not be allowed to stifle a writer's work. Those who cannot defeat them are handicapped and unlikely to reach the heights of their profession.

LEARNING YOUR CRAFT

M S S

Every writer has to learn his craft. Whether that comprises simply being aware of, or competent in, one's chosen language, or studying the structure and composition of the novel form, depends on the individual.

Even subconsciously we have been exposed to language, to writing, all our lives. The creative mind absorbs this more than most, and it finds an expression in the written word in some way or another - writing letters, school essays, a little secretive scribbling under the bedclothes, the adolescent poetry. I remain suspicious of writers (and they exist) who boastfully maintain they never bothered to read books, nor wrote a word until one day they sat down and idly penned a masterpiece akin to Shakespeare's.

For most novelists, learning the craft comes from its pursuance. It may mean one, two, even three novels written as 'trial runs' before the process gels and an end product worthy of submission emerges. In that process of exploration, the writer will have learned much about himself, his ability, his confidence, and above all, what he wants to say.

LITERARY PRIZES

F E S

I'm in two minds about these. There is no doubt that the publicity they receive is good for the book trade generally and that means it is good for authors too. On the other hand they can cause disillusionment among the reading public.

I am thinking here about prizes offered to authors whose books are deemed to have 'literary qualities'. Few writers with the ability to tell a powerful story are ever considered for such competitions. This is because the judges almost always come from a rarefied, literary establishment who choose books not for their entertainment value but for their 'literary elegance'. It is highly unlikely that the great story-tellers of the past, like Steinbeck, Dickens, Hemingway and Maugham, would make even the short list today.

In other words, the winning books' contents and their plot structures, when these elements exist at all, are not designed to please the public but to please the writers themselves. In the main they are self-indulgent books.

The effect is not good for the book trade. With the winner and the short list hyped to the skies, thousands of people rush out to buy these books, only to discover they are bored stiff before they have reached page twenty.

I haven't the same objection to competitions that choose novels on their story-telling and entertainment qualities because they are less likely to disappoint the public. Nevertheless, with taste such a subjective thing, I can't help asking myself how judges decide that this or that book is better than its peers. With millions of people out there, all with different opinions and viewpoints, how do they face the responsibility? What criteria do they use? One of these days I must seek one out and ask him.

M S S

There are so many of these, particularly in the American market, that one can hardly keep track of them. Although it can be said that they encourage the submission of books, do they encourage the writing of books for the reading public?

That latter fact would be hard to judge, given that the general reader, who is after all the consumer, plays no part in the process. The judgement of books, made from the exclusivity of ivory towers, or from the standpoint of marketing managers, does nothing to foster the wellbeing of the novel today.

Worse still for the writing profession, the public wrangling of judges and the sycophantic speeches of award ceremonies are becoming more and more suspect in the public's eye. No single book is worth so much media attention - at the expense of the many other good novels on offer, but ignored in the melée.

For the recipient of such a prize it can prove a double edged sword - a very great encouragement and confirmation of his talent but one tinged, particularly for the first-time novelist, with the uneasy worry that the next book won't live up to the great expectations of him.

MULTIPLE SUBMISSIONS

F E S

The question here is whether an author, who has just finished his book, should send it to only one publisher or to many.

I believe he should send it to as many publishers as he has copies, always provided he tells each one what he is doing. Publishers don't like multiple submissions, of course, because if another publisher beats them to an acceptance, they have paid their readers for nothing.

But I must remind publishers that they do exactly the same thing themselves when they put up a book for auction. They don't offer it to this or that publisher and wait weeks or months for a decision. They put it up for grabs and the highest bidder gets it. The same procedure pertains to any other product in a market economy. So why should writers live under different rules?

In fact, publishers have only themselves to blame for this growing rebellion among authors. If publishers had been more efficient in handling scripts and paid more attention to their authors' interests, we in turn might have shown more patience with them. As things are, what are we supposed to do after investing a year or more of our lives in a book and then be left waiting months for a decision? Starve? Go out in the streets and sell newspapers?

For some full-time writers the situation can be that serious. After all, it is not unusual for even a good book to go to five or six publishers before it is taken. If each one takes four months to make up his mind, twenty months to two years might pass before the author has even a smell of a return on his investment. If he has a family to keep, the effect can be disastrous.

If, however, he approaches four or even half a dozen publishers at the same time, he has dramatically shortened his waiting time.

But what if more than one publisher makes an offer for the book is the question that beginners always ask. The answer is beautifully simple. You do what the publishers do themselves. You offer the book to the highest bidder.

M S S

The norm today is for publishers to treat a novel as a 'product' to be marketed. As this is the practice, publishers should also expect that the author treats his novel in exactly the same way. In other words, he is able to offer his completed manuscript for sale to as many prospective purchasers as possible (or he can afford), all at the same time.

In no other sector of legitimate business does the vendor covertly seek out a single buyer. Would a car salesman invite one person into the back room to view the latest model, whilst firmly shutting the door to other viewers? No. So why should an author be expected to?

The only caution is that of courtesy. An author should tell a publisher that he is seeing a *copy* of the manuscript, not the single original.

NOTEBOOKS: A WRITER'S MUST?

M S S

Writers should be compulsive scribblers and should never travel without the means of writing or recording. Every impression, every interesting snatch of conversation, every sudden flash of inspiration, should be captured instantly! Otherwise, sure as eggs are eggs, it will be forgotten.

Carry a notebook, filofax, or simply a pencil and the back of a bus ticket. Many ideas for stories and novels occur at inconvenient moments - but a few lines in a notebook will jog the memory later. The more interesting snippets can be copied into an ideas file for future use.

PUBLIC LENDING RIGHTS

F E S

PLR, as it is generally known, began payments in 1983 and is a godsend to writers. Each year a certain number of public libraries - it began at around twenty and has now reached thirty - record the total issues for each book title. A central computer then grosses up these figures by the number of public libraries in the country. This number is then multiplied by the Rate per Loan, which is obtained by dividing the government sum allocated by the total number of loans.

The sum paid out per loan varies from year to year but averages out around 1.30 pence per loan. The sum total of a writer's loans are multiplied by this figure and every February he receives his appropriate cheque.

Thus PLR has at last quelled authors' legitimate protests that their work could be read free by any member of the public whereas artists like musicians obtained royalties whenever their work was performed.

The money received is no fortune. The limit any writer can receive at the moment is £6,000 and only sixty or so writers fall into this category. Many receive less than £500 and over 50 per cent less than £100.

Nevertheless, in a profession that has always been badly paid, it helps struggling writers to survive when they might otherwise go under. It is also supremely important in establishing that writers, like other members of the community, have a right to be paid something, however little, when the public make use of their work.

Once an author's book is published, he should apply for registration to: The Registrar, PLR, Bayheath House, Prince Regent Street, Stockton-on-Tees, Cleveland TS18 1DF.

PORTRAYING GOOD AND EVIL

M S S

Perhaps it is the darker side of man's nature coming to the fore, but he certainly has a preference to live the evil life vicariously. Isn't that why the truly nasty villains are remembered - albeit romanticised? Isn't it also true that the patently worthy person who never sins is such a bore to read about?

Even in the most romantic of fairy tales the baddies appear, as they must, if there is to be conflict. But, unless the novel is to be allowed to lapse into melodrama, there can be no all-black or all-white characters. Even the villainous monster must have a soft spot for his old mother; even the saintly paragon must have a lapse into temper or tell the occasional fib.

F E S

It's perhaps fortunate for authors that good people do have their faults, otherwise books about them would make extremely colourless reading. At the same time, imbuing them with imperfections while still giving them an overall impression of virtue, is extremely difficult to do, and probably explains why novels about truly good people are relatively uncommon.

It is a subject that interests me because before I began writing my novel THE TORMENTED, I realised that my main character John Mason, with his basic pacifist beliefs and his ultimate and terrible sacrifice, was really a modern saint. How, then, was I going to make him the vital dynamic figure that the plot required?

It was not easy selecting his imperfections because I realised they might turn some readers against him. Nor is it for me to say whether I chose well or not. But the selection was a challenge in itself and the reviews, particularly one from the Christian Press, did suggest that Mason's faults were forgiven when weighed against his sacrifice.

PRESS OR PUBLICITY AGENCIES

F E S

These are institutions whose purpose is to obtain publicity for anyone requesting it. It might surprise beginners to learn that much of the news about actors, pop stars, celebrities, and even well-known authors, is paid for in hard cash, but it is a fact of life.

An author might get this help in one of two ways. If he is lucky enough, his publisher might pay the fees for him, although publishers usually have their own publicity departments whose degree of success usually depends on the money allocated to them.

The other way is for the author to pay for the publicity himself. Unless he has more money than sense, however, he would be most unwise to do this because, for an unknown author, it is highly unlikely that the extra sales the publicity gains for him will go anywhere near to meeting his agency's fees.

However, there is no doubt that high-pressure publicity will sell almost anything, and the fact publishers spend huge sums on certain books makes their claim that books sell by word of mouth and not by advertising look very frail indeed. It also explains why the occasional rich author, as well as the fading celebrity or film star, is sometimes able to keep his name in the public eye when his recent works have lost their sparkle. Although it might be hotly denied, it happens, and will continue to happen in a world where money can shape public taste.

PSEUDONYMS

M S S

If you have a fairly common name there is some merit in adopting a less common one, to avoid confusing readers. Also, there is often with authors, myself included, a sense of not being at ease having one's name in the public domain.

With poetry and journalism I have always written under my own name, perhaps because of the more factual nature of such work. With fiction I lean toward the use of a pseudonym, as it feels more comfortable for me. That, I suspect, is the actress in me wanting to hide behind a character - only this character is an author rather than a stage persona.

F E S

Another word for these is pen names. They are used for a number of reasons, sometimes to disguise the writer's true identity, sometimes to hide a more ordinary name, and sometimes to help classify one type of an author's work from another.

In my case I have only used one pen name, David Farrell. Many years ago I was invited to write a few serials for women's magazines, and with the film of my book, 633 SQUADRON, just appearing, it was felt the contrast between the two types of story was too great for them both to appear under the same name. All in all, I used this pseudonym for six serials which later were published as novels.

The reason I have used Frederick E Smith for the great majority of my novels is because, when I began writing, I had a half-baked idea that if I could get my work published under Smith, there could be no question of its being accepted for any other reason than its worth. Whereas if I used some glamorous name, I could never be absolutely certain of this. I suppose the Yorkshireman in me over-reacts to ostentation.

Today I often regret using Smith. People do tend to connote quality with exclusivity. Also, a common name is, ironically, more difficult to remember, and so I have the suspicion the titles of my books tend to be remembered rather than their author.

PUBLISHING CONGLOMERATES

F E S

There is a trend today for conglomerates to take over publishing houses (which in itself suggests publishing is a profitable enterprise). Whether this trend will benefit authors or be to their disadvantage is difficult to judge at the moment. On the one hand it should mean more efficiency in production and marketing, which ought to lead to greater royalties for authors. On the other hand, conglomerates might favour only best selling books with the highest profit margin, which would be a disaster for good literature.

M S S

On every street corner are proclamations from publishing houses that 'things have never been so bad'. Is this why, one is tempted to ask, mergers and takeover bids are the order of the day? One suspects the profit motive operates more so than altruism, as each successive acquisition is quickly carved up and sold on.

It becomes increasingly more difficult to track who owns whom as the multi-nationals buy first this, then that smaller specialist publisher. And equally so, when a conglomerate is in ownership, the volume of products (in this case books) increases, but the range of choice becomes narrower. In other words, the razzamataz and glitz up front squanders money on a handful of flagship names, at the expense of all the equally good writers who are left starving in the bilges.

I have never been a subscriber to the 'big is beautiful' theme because, unrestrained, it is bad business for all concerned. When the hierarchy of a company can change twice in a year, and authors are axed at the drop of a hat as each new broom editor makes his mark, where is the stability and loyalty the literary profession needs if it is to survive with integrity?

REVIEWS

M S S

Good, bad or indifferent, we love or hate them. An author may well preen at a selection of laudations from critics. But then he should put them from his mind, for fear of inflating his ego.

The bad criticism or, worse still, the indifferent, can destroy confidence and plunge a writer into a near suicidal decline. There is only one answer - ignore them. Remember, they are one person's opinion. For every review which damns your characterisation, you may well find one which praises just that facet.

If your book is published, then both author and publisher had faith in it. If the public read it, that's the best review of all.

F E S

These can be obtained by an author in two ways. Either by his paying a Press Cutting Agency to scan the newspapers and journals and send him the relevant reviews of his latest book, or by leaving it to his publisher, who usually has an account with an agency, to forward copies to him.

As Press Cutting Agencies are quite expensive these days, the temptation is to leave the task to one's publisher. The problem here is that one usually has to rely on a junior member of the publisher's staff to do the forwarding, and so it is quite possible a writer will receive only a percentage of the reviews his book has earned.

Not that this is any serious loss. The day of the great reviewers are long over. Few newspapers give more than a few column inches to book reviews, which means only a few of the hundred books published every week receive a mention.

For those that do, the results can be disappointing. Apart from the quality newspapers and one or two of the tabloids, cub reporters are often used as reviewers, particularly in provincial newspapers. They in turn, to save themselves having to read the books, often simply re-write the blurb.

This has little or no effect on sales, however. Many of the best sellers never get a mention in the Press, while books which devour far more than their share of column inches often sell fewer than two thousand copies. The general public, it seems, seldom read or take notice of book reviews.

Yet many authors, particularly beginners, wait for their reviews as anxiously as actresses after their first night, and some go into deep depressions when their book is criticised. Let them be reassured that (a) bad reviews will not harm the book sales if the publisher has done his job well, and (b) for every bad review it is likely there will soon be one praising the book to the skies. 'What is one man's meat is another man's poison' might have been written for the book trade.

SNOBBERY IN THE LITERARY WORLD

M S S

Today more than ever, due in no small part to marketing ploys, the novel is being forced into two camps - the literary and the looked-down upon.

The latter category embraces the so-called women's romantic fiction, westerns, and certain types of war or crime stories. It is true that these forms are in essence lighter in tone and slighter in content, yet they have the bigger readership. Those who have tried unsuccessfully to break into the Mills and Boon format can testify to the difficulty there is in writing such apparently 'easy' books. They have, in their way, as much to state of the human condition as any other form does. Perhaps even more so, as the characters in them are readily identifiable and sympathised with.

In the literary camp there would seem to be at present a growing tendency towards the incomprehensible. A novel may be more than an imaginative story, it may aim at leading a reader into self-discovery on important issues, yet none of this makes an enduring novel if it is not accessible. Books glorifying books, extolling the virtues of psychological consciousness, and ethnic duplicity, may be well written but speak at no greater volume to the readership.

The myth that only the academic literary novel has any enduring worth is one fostered by its breeding ground. The University hierarchy is, I'm afraid, self-perpetuating by creating its own myths.

TELEVISION: A DEATH KNELL TO LITERATURE?

F E S

It appears to do no damage to non-fiction; indeed some programmes are said to increase book sales. But I think it endangers imaginative literature. Before television, when children were entertained by books and the radio, their imagination was called on to a considerable degree. It was a stimulus that helped the imagination to develop, and enabled the adolescent, and eventually the adult, to appreciate literature that called for reader participation, in other words the better type of literature.

Television, by presenting the images instead of suggesting them, has greatly reduced the call on the imagination. Too much is given the viewer and consequently too much is taken away. The child's imagination suffers and quality books become difficult to read. In fact, the sight of grown men reading comics, which is not an unusual sight these days, suggests *any* book is becoming hard to read. I understand that entire novels written in comic strip form are now being published in the United States. One finds it difficult to blame anything but television for this trend.

UNITED STATES COPYRIGHT

F E S

The length of a book's copyright in the United States is now only twenty-eight years after its first date of publication in its country of origin. This took effect from the 31st December 1977. It can be extended for another 28 years but only by its author making his claim before the period of grace runs out. To obtain full details, authors should apply to: The Renewals Section, Register of Copyrights, Library of Congress, Washington DC 20559, USA.

VANITY PUBLISHING

F E S

I don't care for it for a number of reasons. Far too many poor books are being published already for the health of writers and the book trade in general. Some are so badly written they would have been tossed on the slush pile twenty years ago: in fact they are a disgrace to the publishers who print them. To add even more books - books that even these publishers would not accept - can only suffocate the market further.

As for the writers who pay for their own publication (unless they are among the rare few who have something so interesting to say that it blinds publishers to its worth), they are only deceiving themselves as to their true talent. To test himself, a writer must dive into the big pond and take his chances. To paddle about in a tiny, home-made pond is to live a life of self-delusion.

M S S

Beware the adverts soliciting manuscripts and guaranteeing publication. Any novel submitted will be praised in glowing terms that imply the reputable publishing houses must be mad to refuse it. However, if you have several hundred, if not thousands, of pounds to risk, then by all means accept the temptation to see yourself in print - at your own expense.

At your expense it will be, as the vanity publisher will print only a limited number of copies and bind even less. He will do no marketing, so the chances of your book appearing for the public are nil. Having paid out, say, £5,000 you could be faced with almost as much again if you want to 'buy' the remaining copies before they are pulped.

Self publication is a different matter altogether. Having expended your own money on having the work printed, you do the marketing, you control the copies. Unfortunately, novels rarely achieve success in this way, except for a very limited localised market when, for example, it may indirectly chronicle the life and times of a village. Non-fiction stands a much better chance this way.

WRITER'S BLOCK

M S S

Mention of this is at worst akin to visitation by The Dark Night of the Soul, and at best the writing equivalent of the common cold - nearly all of us catch it from time to time.

There comes to most writers that morning when the blank white sheet in the typewriter stays that way, or the story stagnates at a point when it won't progress. What's to do?

Giving the sub-conscious the task of sorting it out, while you walk the dog or relax with a cup of coffee may get most writers over the simple problem with words. For those struggling with the plot or the creation of the story there are two alternatives that work well.

Confront the characters with an unexpectedly explosive happening. How will they react now? What twists and changes does it produce in the story? Or, look objectively at the characters created. They should be 'real' people to you, so ask them: "What would you do now?" The answers may surprise you!

F E S

At the risk of sounding a humbug, I must confess I've never suffered from it. Unless, of course, it means the problem of finding the correct word or sentence. Everyone suffers that, and I usually overcome it quite quickly by using the subconscious, as I explained earlier in the book.

But if it means drying up either in the middle of a novel or being unable to think of a subject for a new one, then I can honestly say I've never known either. If I have a problem halfway through a novel, it is the difficulty of selecting the right path from the number available rather than finding no path at all. As for subjects, there seem so many fascinating ones in the world, that I can't understand a writer being unable to find one that grips his imagination.

WRITERS' CIRCLES

F E S

I think they can be a help in some ways. Writing is a lonely occupation and it often helps novice writers to mix with their peers and to share their disappointments and successes. It can also be a help when the circles invite professional people to give lectures.

But they serve little value when they criticise one another's manuscripts. This is so often the case of the blind leading the blind and giving one another advice that is either misleading or outdated. On such evenings novices are better employed at home learning their craft by writing. There is no substitute for that.

M S S

Most smaller clubs simply don't have the financial wherewithal to invite experienced professional writers to talk on aspects of writing. But they do provide a forum for socialising with people who have writers' minds. For make no mistake, the minds of writers are somewhat different from the general population's, and the chance to speak freely on matters of concern can be a refreshing and stimulating exercise.

The novice can also derive some benefit from the exercise of entering any competitions the club runs. The discipline of producing a range of material, to a deadline, can be effective training indeed.

WRITING CONFERENCES

M S S

These can vary in length from a single day seminar, to a long weekend, to a full week, non-residential or residential - take your pick. Your choice depends on your pocket, available time, and your inclination to mix with fairly large numbers of like-minded individuals.

As interchanges of ideas and 'it happened to me' stories, they can be quite an escape valve for a writer closeted in the narrow world of his own room. Techniques can be learned, and speakers listened to. All of this will stimulate the imagination, but won't write the book for you.

There are two dangers to be aware of. Firstly, the beginner can come away from a first conference with a feeling akin to despair.

He has seen all these *great writers* and is convinced he will never mount their exalted pedestal! Nonsense, of course. Writers are the same mixture of humanity as any other professional group: some will quietly dispense wisdom, some will riotously blow their own trumpets.

Secondly, one can all too easily become a professional conference attender and not a professional writer.

F E S

There is no doubt that writers' conferences are pleasant occasions to attend and, for both novices and experienced writers alike it is refreshing to hear that others experience the same problems. They are also venues where writers can learn in private conversations whether so-and-so is a good agent and whether so-and-so publisher gives one a fair deal.

But their very charm can deceive a novice into thinking that he is already breaking into the world of writing. He must realise that swanning about with experienced writers does not make him any more of a writer than the electrician who is servicing the dining room refrigerator. One learns to write by writing and an honest novice will soon realise that while one or even two conferences a year will do him no harm, the rest of the time he spends on them would be better employed by slaving over his typewriter, less glamorous though this might be.

WRITING SCHOOLS AND TUTORS

M S S

As both a tutor for a leading Writers' College, as well as a private assessor of individual manuscripts, I must declare an interest here.

There is certainly a place for both schools and tutors. Each will help a beginner to correct faulty grammar and syntax, point out flaws in his construction, sharpen his technique, and steer him in the right direction. Moreover professional criticism, by giving an objective assessment of his work, will give a novice more confidence in his talent.

At the same time, an honest school or tutor will never claim to make every pupil a successful writer. As stated earlier, the talent must be there at the outset. If it is, then capable professional tuition can do nothing but good.

Final Thoughts

To be a good novelist one needs a fertile and inventive mind, for not only does a writer have to find ideas but he needs to both invent and solve problems as he writes. And while the invention of problems can be exacting enough, the solving of them can sometimes be diabolically difficult.

Then he has to make that cold synopsis spring into vibrant life. He has to lift those flat words from their paper and make them three dimensional. He has to make them glow with life so that for a while the reader is living with his creation.

To do this he should read his words as if he were the reader himself. He should ask himself if the words move him. If they bring tears to his eyes, he should be proud, not ashamed. For if he cries, his readers will cry too. He should never be ashamed of emotion because it is his stock in trade.

If he is aiming for the stars, I also believe he should not put cruel wit or malice into his work unless it is to illustrate and emphasise their sterility. Instead he should use humour, sympathy, and understanding. It is these aspects that so often determine the quality of a book because it is not only writing skill that turns an everyday theme into a work of art but the sensitivity and compassion of its writer.

For all these reasons and others I believe lecturers and anyone who writes books of this nature should be honest with novices and tell them that although advice can be very useful and can cut corners for them, it cannot by itself make them into successful writers. Talent, imagination, determination and other essential factors we have discussed are either in a man or they are not. If a novice has the gift of self-criticism, he will soon find out the truth about himself.

At the same time, whether the novice is a natural artist or not, or whether he gets published or not, he has a great deal to gain from writing. I mentioned earlier how it can increase one's tolerance. That is no small thing but the benefits do not end there.

I have often thought that writing is one of the few pursuits in life that enables a man or woman to make something worthwhile out of their disappointments and tragedies. To most people such events often seem pointless and leave their lives poorer. But a writer can use his misfortunes to give his work more depth and compassion. The tragedy that once seemed so senseless can now gain a meaning if it is used to bring relief and comfort to himself and others.

Novels do not need to be published to do this. If they are read only by one's family and friends, they can still serve this purpose. And if they do that, might they not have achieved more than any banal best seller?

Success has many paths and many interpretations, and every writer, novice and professional alike, would be wise to bear this in mind and never let his life be afflicted by either success or failure. They are, after all, both imposters.

Frederick E Smith

Appendix

Useful Books for the Writer's Desk

1 A dictionary: the most comprehensive one you can afford. Words are your stock in trade - be accurate.

2 A Thesaurus. Roget's is perhaps the most well known, but there are now similar (and easier to access) volumes available. Such books assist in the finding of synonyms and antonyms and are an absolute must for any writer.

3 A work of grammar and English usage: such as Fowler's Modern English Usage or The Oxford Guide to English Language.

4 Brewer's Dictionary of Phrase and Fable.

5 A classical dictionary.

6 Dictionaries of quotations and proverbs.

7 Pan Books of Names. These are published in separate editions for girls and boys.

8 The Writers' and Artists' Year Book and/or The Writers' Handbook.

9 An encyclopedia: the latest possible single-volume edition from a specialist publishing house.

10 An Atlas of the Modern World. Boundaries and names change rapidly, but topography can be checked.

NOTES

NOTES

NOTES

NOTES

NOTES

NOTES